FOR THE YOUNG VIEWER

RALPH GARRY, Professor of Educational Psychology at Boston University, has been actively concerned for the past decade with programming for children in both commercial and noncommercial broadcasting. In 1957 and again in 1962, Dr. Garry was the editor of two booklets entitled *Television for Children,* published by the Foundation for Character Education.

* * *

FREDERICK B. RAINSBERRY has been associated in an executive capacity with children's programming at the Canadian Broadcasting Corporation since 1954 and is currently National Supervisor of School Broadcasts. Between 1940 and 1954, Dr. Rainsberry taught at high schools in Canada, at Springfield College and at Michigan State University.

* * *

CHARLES WINICK, a psychologist, has taught at the University of Rochester, MIT, and Columbia University. He has conducted research on how children use mass media, preschoolers' games, student-teacher relations, children's humor, fan mail, and the development of religious ideas in young people. His publications include *Trends in Human Relations Research* (1955) and *Taste and the Censor in Television* (1955).

FOR THE YOUNG VIEWER

TELEVISION PROGRAMMING FOR CHILDREN...AT THE LOCAL LEVEL

Edited by
RALPH GARRY * F. B. RAINSBERRY
CHARLES WINICK

McGRAW-HILL BOOK COMPANY, INC.
New York / Toronto / London

Foreword

Certain words evoke powerful emotional responses. Many of them, even when used independently of each other, have the capacity to evoke such responses for predictable groups of our society.

However, there are two words, *children* and *television,* which, when juxtaposed, have a very special and universal impact.

This book is for all those who hold a prime concern with improving children or television — or both. It is for broadcasters and parents, creators of programs and educators.

It has been made possible through the active cooperation of the 252 broadcasters who responded to one more *"won't you please fill in this questionnaire"* request. We are grateful to all of them.

But the objective of the Television Information Office in this undertaking reaches out beyond a mere description of ideas and formats that broadcasters might find useful in their own programming for children. The goal is to extend knowledge of children and children's programs beyond the range readily available to most laymen.

If this reach has not too far exceeded the grasp, it is due in considerable measure to the generous contributions of time, energy, and expert knowledge of the three men who steered this publication between the obvious and the obscure: Dr. Ralph Garry of Boston University, Dr. F. B. Rainsberry of the Canadian Broadcasting Corporation, and Dr. Charles Winick of Columbia University.

We hope that the information and observations presented here will help to advance the goals of all who maintain a continuing interest in the interaction between television and the children who turn to it for stimulation, information, and recreation.

LOUIS HAUSMAN, Director
Television Information Office

v

Contents

Introduction

Many diversified groups combine to form the audience of any television station. One of the most diverse groups in any community is made up of the children who eagerly watch television. Children vary widely in age, interests, degree of maturity, personality, and background; these variations determine the use that children make of television and what they take away from any viewing experience. Identifying and satisfying the needs of the large numbers of children in his audience are among the major responsibilities of the local broadcaster.

The task of programming for children is at once the easiest and the hardest to fulfill: *easiest* because the enormous curiosity of children and their interest in the adult world prompt them to view almost anything; *hardest* because of the many different levels of maturation to be found in a youthful audience.

Where does a conscientious broadcaster get ideas for programs as he goes about the job of satisfying his young viewers? If he turns to textbooks or specialists he will get scant comfort; the ideas found there are often vague and only suggestive, mainly because people who know about children are accustomed neither to thinking about how to program for them nor to operating a television station.

This book evolved from a desire to assist broadcasters and program producers in developing programs for children *at the local level* by suggesting ideas that would help them use their traditional early morning, late afternoon, and weekend children's hours to greatest advantage. Station managers will find descriptions of what their fellow-broadcasters are doing *in their own communities*. The purpose is not to provide a catalog, but to stimulate consideration of the wide variety of ways in which children's programs can be designed and, by this, to spur and facilitate the creative efforts of those responsible for such programming.

1

In another sense there is a second, related purpose: We hope that the information presented here will serve as a stimulus to creative people outside broadcasting in their efforts to satisfy the manifold interests of children and that their talents may be enlisted in the task of programming for children.

Gathering the Data

For the Young Viewer began with a three-page questionnaire, six copies of which were sent to all television stations in the United States, noncommercial as well as commercial. The stations were asked to provide descriptions of their locally produced programs designed for at-home viewing by children between the ages of four and twelve. Programs designed primarily for use in schools or as an integral part of the school curriculum were specifically excluded as were programs consisting entirely of syndicated films. Responses to the questionnaire were received from 252 stations (44 per cent of those queried); 223 of these stations provided the information for the 425 programs described in this report. As the responses came in, the staff of the Television Information Office transferred précis descriptions of each program to 5- by 8-inch cards with no identifying information as to station or city of origin.

A number of the programs reported were one-time broadcasts. Most, however, were series of longer duration. Reflecting the diversity of their intended audiences, they ranged from preschool interests to those of adolescents, from Bible stories to state fairs. The diversity in programs was a surprise. Even the junior variety show—a basic format for many stations—contained many elements testifying to the imaginativeness of the producers.

Just as surprising as the diversity of the programs was the diversity of the originating stations—in geographical distribution, size of station staff, and extent of community resources. The 223 stations represent 146 different areas, and a scanning of the programs selected for detailed description shows that they come from communities ranging in size from 68,000 television homes to those with more than 5 million. Network-affiliated, network-owned, unaffiliated commercial, and ETV stations all produced their share of these programs.

Grouping the Programs

The two main tasks facing the committee of editors were to impose some order on the program information provided by the stations and to establish a basis for selecting programs for detailed description. Using the précis cards prepared by the staff, each member of the committee made a selection of programs. From the pooling of these selections came the order and arrangement of the programs that follow.

As we compared judgments we found ourselves using two sets of standards in selection. The first was *feasibility* for a broadcaster, the second was *desirability* for children. Feasibility implies that the program was suited to the resources of typical stations with regard to money, staff time, equipment, and community resources. Desirability indicates an appeal to children (rather than adults) and a contribution to children in terms of the information, skill, entertainment, imagination, variety, or originality reflected. For these reasons, fewer programs utilizing familiar formats such as the television kindergarten or the junior variety show have received detailed descriptions than their numerical abundance might have suggested.

We freely admit the selections are arbitrarily made on a subjective basis. Another group would have performed differently. We would probably have made different selections had we actually seen each program, but we would have been introducing value judgments as to the quality of production. In effect, we assumed each program was well produced, limiting our selection to the indicated program content. In spite of the relatively crude means of selection, there was a high degree of agreement within the committee and it was this agreement that determined which programs are described in detail. In a few instances where two programs of unusual interest were much alike, the decision for detailed description was based on the adequacy of the information available. For this reason, many of the programs that received only brief descriptions contain valuable ideas for children's programs, even though we know little more about the program than is contained in the short description.

Our first effort at grouping the programs was by content, but this proved unwieldy. What gradually emerged were five categories that basically indicate the purpose of the program. Many of the programs were directed at having the child explore, to enlist his curiosity in new things, whether people or places, objects or events. Another set of programs aimed at getting children to do things, to develop new skills, and to try new experiences. By classifying the programs according to what appeared to be their intent, we arrived at five categories, which we have called "Exploration," "Doing," "Storytelling," "Orientation," and "Multipurpose" programs.

From the broadcaster's viewpoint, there is a certain functional utility in this classification scheme. We customarily think of children's programs in terms of age levels. Yet this is unwieldy because, with the exception of preschoolers, there is rarely a time when one age group is present to watch programs to the exclusion of other age levels. Furthermore, the age grouping ignores differences in maturational levels and in interests of children. Our categories have placed the emphasis on the *activities* of children. This, in turn, is likely to be a more practical consideration both in regard to production problems and audience appeal. Not all of the programs fitted neatly into our categories, with the result that some were placed in the group which seemed best to describe their primary purpose.

More Than a Catalog

Several additional elements are included. At the beginning of each of the five program sections, a commentary will be found that covers a number of aspects of programming and production: determining program objectives and content, camera treatment, pace of program, and the like. Dr. Frederick Rainsberry has drawn on his long experience with the Canadian Broadcasting Corporation in both entertainment and educational broadcasting for children for these observations, which relate to the specific type of program in each section.

Dr. Charles Winick has contributed a section, "The World of the Young Viewer," that deals directly with children—their development, needs, reactions—and with some psychological considerations to be taken into account in programming for children. In his essay, Dr. Winick attempts to translate what is known about child development into terms meaningful to a broadcaster. One difficulty facing those who program

4

for children is that adults have forgotten their own childhood. Slow, imperceptible growth has erased the impressions and perceptions of childhood, and rarely do adults get close enough to their children's lives to recapture them. Dr. Winick first draws a series of contrasts that distinguish the reactions of the child from those of the adult, then calls attention to several important aspects of development and shows how these yield differential reactions at different age levels. He closes by showing their relationship to a number of specific aspects of programming.

Some of the emotional responses of children are not dealt with specifically. These have been deliberately omitted because the main focus of this publication is on useful program ideas. Moreover, a number of the sources listed in the Reference section will provide this information for the broadcaster. In planning a program for children, the broadcaster must identify for himself his purposes and objectives in the program and give serious consideration to the attitudes and values being developed or reinforced.

A selected bibliography of sources of information about film material suitable for use in programming for children is also included in References.

Speaking of resources, one of the most interesting discoveries of the survey was the great range of resources being tapped for program materials in many communities. It is not unusual to find schools, libraries, and public service organizations cooperating in programs for children. This barely begins the list, for we found historical societies, art galleries, zoologists, kennel clubs, foresters, missile manufacturers and speech therapists among the resources being utilized for programs for children.

The information and ideas contained in *For the Young Viewer* are, therefore, the work of many people. To all of them, known and unknown, the editors give thanks. We wish to express appreciation to the staff of the Television Information Office for invaluable assistance in the preparation of this volume, and particularly to Lawrence Creshkoff, TIO's executive editor. He contributed a number of the detailed program descriptions as well as many thoughtful recommendations. We especially acknowledge the fundamental contributions of the station managers and production personnel who not only conceived and developed the programs described here, but who took the time to answer the questions we asked about their programming for children. In a very real sense this is their book.

RALPH GARRY
For the editors

Boston, Massachusetts
June, 1962

Exploration

Children love to explore. They begin with their bodies, expand to ash-trays and silverware as soon as they can reach, to rooms and stairs and garden paths as soon as they can crawl, to the neighborhood when they can walk and run.

Television can take them out of the neighborhood to anywhere in the world, to any time and place in history. Through these programs children visit other countries and see their customs and practices; they meet other people, some famous, some ordinary; they participate in historic events. These are programs that shape interests and expand horizons.

Motion picture film fits naturally into such programs. Many stations have shown creative imagination by taking the viewers into the surrounding area, into the forest, the factory, and the streets to show children the world about them.

I am a part of all that I have met;
Yet all experience is an arch wherethro'
Gleams that untravell'd world, whose margin fades
Forever and forever when I move.

Tennyson, *Ulysses*

By means of exploration children acquire vast stores of information and learn how to use it. Exploration is a voyage of discovery wherein children find new facts, new lands, new people, and in the end find out more about themselves. We talk much about documentary programs for adults by means of which we continue our education informally throughout our adult lives. Travel films, an evening with friends spent in viewing color slides, the reading of nonfiction, and much radio listening or television viewing all afford enriching recreation.

Children like documentary programs because they are curious about the world around them, and they will quickly be attracted to any medium which enables them to explore a new world and to have adventures that may not be possible for them in the normal course of their daily lives. In the development of documentary material for children, many program directors like to present programs on natural science. The main hazard here is that the specialist in this field may himself not understand children. His information may be responsible and his presentation competent from an adult point of view while children may not respond to him at all.

Beyond the personality of the presenter himself, it is imperative that the producer endeavor to see the information that he would present as children themselves would see it naturally. The producer often seems to be more concerned with the landscape than in planning close-ups of the natural life about which the presenter is speaking. In the adventure of a nature hike the children themselves should receive some direction from their guide. At the same time, they like to discover for themselves some of the phenomena of nature that are shown on the program. Mr.

Wizard frequently allows his young assistant to share in his physics experiments. The program director should always know that such participation invites the most intense identification by the young viewers in their homes.

A science program can be greatly enhanced by the proper balance of documentary film that has been shot specially for the occasion or procured from a film distributor. Simple animations representational of natural processes that need slowing down or speeding up in order to be observed are very helpful. This material may be combined with the studio presentation, which allows for close-ups of the animals, plants, or laboratory models that are to be inspected.

Many television producers have successfully adapted the television camera to the microscope in order to give, in full-screen size, the image seen by the scientist through the eye of the microscope itself. Such suggestions as these indicate the practical ways in which the producer can solve his problem in terms of television production while he ensures a responsible and interesting presentation for his young viewers.

Journeys or visits to foreign lands make good material for children's television. Children enjoy learning about the ways of life of children in other lands. One of the most useful ways of presenting information of this kind is through film. The program director should recognize at the outset that to substitute an unedited educational film for a television program is not likely to make good television, since the film was made for showing under very different circumstances. Here the challenge to the producer lies in careful editing of the film to be matched with a studio presentation.

Another problem arises in the use of studio guests to help illustrate life in other countries. Let us suppose that the producer wants to introduce his audience to a family that has recently come from a foreign land. He must spend a great deal of time orienting the family to the studio situation so that its unfamiliarity will not spoil their normal, natural conversation nor in any way impede their desire to express pride in their native land. In addition, such orientation enables the producer to select those events and that information for which he can provide the most suitable visual presentation. It is important for the young viewer that he see the costumes and other objects that he would not normally see. A good balance of film and studio presentation ensures a wide scope for the experience of the young viewer within the maximum time available.

In seeking areas and subjects for exploration by the very youngest children, it is important to begin where they are ready to start—close to home. Just as the early stages of the curriculum at most schools begin with the exploration of the local community, so the television programs can lead children to a new appreciation of the zoo or the nearby nature trail. With the understanding guidance of a sensitive leader, the lure of exploration can be the arch of experience that makes growth into adulthood rich and inviting.

Dateline Boston
Boston, Massachusetts

One dilemma facing broadcasters in programming for children arises from the tendency of all but the very youngest children to choose *adult* programs, rather than those designed specifically for them. DATELINE BOSTON, a 25-minute early evening program, which has been broadcast five times a week since November, 1957, suggests that stimulating television for children can be built into the framework of a family program. Furthermore, this program contains many recurring features directed to children which could be adapted as separate one-time or series programs.

Depending on the subject, this program originates from studio or outside location and is live, on film, or on tape. For one series of 10 programs, "The Children of Asia," a station team spent six weeks shooting film from Karachi, through Burma and Thailand, to Hong Kong and the Philippines to help create greater understanding among children and to show the work of UNICEF in the fight against disease.

A monthly visit to Franklin Park Zoo makes possible a year-round follow-up on the habits and activities of the zoo animals. Once a month a folk singer (who teaches history and literature) sings the folk music of America, with children as his guests. Four times a year the Children's Museum presents an exhibition and demonstration of natural and social history: "Light through the Centuries," "Life in Tibet," "The Egg and You." And, once each week, in "Captain Bob's Adventures in Art," a drawing lesson is presented that is built around a theme, such as the furniture of New England. Each month, "YMCA and YWCA" emphasize physical fitness with children participating.

DATELINE BOSTON is introduced and moderated by a host who has been identified with many of the station's community activities. It is produced in association with the Massachusetts Department of Education, and makes use of the resources of over 150 cooperating local and regional organizations.

Gypsy's World
Seattle, Washington

During the period of the first three grades in school, children begin to be conscious of national differences in dress, architecture, facial characteristics. They are fascinated by Dutch shoes, straw huts on stilts, the differences between Western and Oriental eye structure. Often this is when they begin either to welcome or distrust such differences.

The theme of GYPSY'S WORLD, a weekly Friday evening quarter-hour program, is that much is to be learned from travel, from seeing and enjoying how others live, from recognizing the similarities as well as the differences between "our" way and "theirs." Gypsy acts out make-believe trips in her gaily decorated wagon, going from one country to another, investigating the folklore, customs, music, and dancing.

In a four-program sequence on Italy, Gypsy first arrives in Italy and stops her wagon in a forest outside of Rome. She tells an old Italian folk tale. The following week she goes into a theatre in a small Italian town and sees a group of dancers rehearsing. She watches them, then asks them to explain the steps and the meaning of the dances. An Italian family invites Gypsy to their home. After dinner they sit in the garden and sing. They explain the music to Gypsy. Finally, Gypsy leaves Italy in her wagon. She passes along the Italian Riviera and tells a story about people in this part of the country.

Gypsy spends some seven hours in preparation for each 15-minute program; the set designer, four hours; and the director, two hours. The number of participants varies, depending on the theme of a particular broadcast.

GYPSY'S WORLD is low-key and relaxed. By staying within a quarter-hour format, the child's attention span is accommodated, and the temptation to crowd too much material into one program is avoided.

Zoorama

San Diego, California

Most young children would happily go to the zoo at least once a week. One problem is that more questions are usually raised than parents can answer. Since 1955 San Diego has solved the problem through a weekly, half-hour, late Saturday afternoon program, ZOORAMA.

Carefully planned with officials of the San Diego Zoological Society, each ZOORAMA broadcast is geared to the current most timely subject matter. The program is prerecorded on video tape, which provides flexibility in production scheduling. Various animals are viewed at their respective mealtimes; the newborn young are captured on tape as they take their first steps.

The program host is accompanied by zoo curators, who provide information about the animals being visited. The hyrax, a small animal that looks like a rodent, is shown in close-up, and the viewer learns that he is actually most closely related to the elephant—because of his hoof-like foot structure. While watching the spider monkey, he learns the meaning of "prehensile."

The high interest in programming built around the zoo is demonstrated by the fact that ZOORAMA was syndicated in the 1961-to-1962 season to stations in eleven United States cities.

Wondertime
Sacramento, California

All producers of serious children's programs face the problem of achieving unity and educational significance within each program, while taking into account the child's short attention span. WONDERTIME achieves this by developing a single theme for each broadcast, to which a number of seemingly different elements are related. The theme may be seasonal (spring, fall), topical (animals, the weather), or historical (Washington's birthday).

A program at the beginning of March opened with the March Hare cavorting about the stage, followed by a passage from *Alice in Wonderland* read by the WONDERTIME hostess, an amiable member of the station staff. Background exposition about March, illustrated by still photographs and flannel-board figures, included the origin of its name (Mars, god of war); the lion-and-lamb myth; birth month of Alexander Graham Bell, Vincent Van Gogh, and Albert Einstein; "The Star-Spangled Banner" officially proclaimed the national anthem.

Following an 11-minute film on March winds, the hostess presented a study of kites of all kinds, which included kite history, kite customs in other lands, their use in meteorology, and the most famous kite experiment of all—Benjamin Franklin's. The demonstration was accompanied by strong warnings about the danger involved in the Franklin experiment together with safety rules for kite-flying.

The program is produced by Sacramento State College under the supervision of a specialist in teacher education. He devised a "Hidden Geography" contest in which viewers compete for prizes, including a set of the *Britannica Junior* encyclopedia.

Each program is recorded on tape for Saturday morning broadcast by the originating station and rebroadcast the following Monday night on the local ETV station.

Children at the Tulsa State Fair

Tulsa, Oklahoma

Television's ability to serve as a contemporary magic carpet for children was demonstrated in three hour-long programs during the Oklahoma State Fair in October, 1961. Through two remote television cameras, video-tape recorder, and film cameras at the fairgrounds, children at home were able to feel that they actually had been to the fair.

Each program consisted of visits to the children's barnyard, to the winning exhibits, and—for just plain fun—to the midway. In the barnyard were found samples of the young of all farm animals: chicks, ducklings, pigs, colts, lambs, calves, and kids. Children who had raised the animals talked about their experiences. Children who had entered the foods, needlecraft, artwork, decorating, and livestock competitions were interviewed. The reactions of children to their first taste and feel of cotton candy, their first "plane ride," and their first attempts to throw darts at balloons were recorded.

By working through such organizations as the Future Farmers of America, the 4-H Clubs, and the Oklahoma State University extension service, the significance of the state fair beyond its carnival aspects was underlined. CHILDREN AT THE TULSA STATE FAIR suggests that there are things happening in the life of every community which children can explore through television (programs by other stations reflect the same awareness) . The arrival of a circus in town; a printing plant; a fork-lift truck in a warehouse; riveters at work on a new building; an automated assembly plant; freight cars being coupled and uncoupled; boats raised and lowered through canal locks; how bricks are made: All these lend themselves to examination by the camera's eye.

Wonderama
New York, New York

For four hours every Sunday (9:00 A.M. to 1:00 P.M.), New York children are offered a major program that combines fun with serious exploration into the worlds of science, travel, theatre, sports, animal life, industry, literature, history, and politics. Guest experts from these fields appear with models or samples of their work or their discoveries. The host serves as a guide rather than as a teacher; he leads the fifty children invited to the weekly taping session to learn about the subjects presented by asking questions rather than being lectured at. Between serious segments of the program, the children in the studio (and home viewers) relax with cartoons and games like "Simon Says."

Other participation activities include spelling bees, instruction in ballroom dancing, etiquette, judo, and wrestling. For special occasions, a WONDERAMA news corps has been developed: A 12-year-old, armed with camera and an official press pass, covered President de Gaulle's visit to New York. Mock presidential primaries were held in 1960, which included recorded messages from the candidates asking for WONDERAMA audience support. To demonstrate the intricacies of United Nations translation procedures, a mock Security Council session was held with four children participating: one from the United States, one from England, one from France, and one from the USSR.

With a major expenditure of time and effort (some 160 man-hours go into the preparation of each program) WONDERAMA uses the facilities available in New York to provide an unusual broadcasting experience for children. Stations in other communities may find ways to adapt the techniques employed here to stimulate as well as to entertain within the resources available to them.

Junior News Review

Binghamton, New York

Teachers of social studies in elementary grades are often handicapped by the need to await the arrival of weekly junior periodicals for their current events classes. JUNIOR NEWS REVIEW presents news and interpretation for the 6- to 12-year-old every Monday through Friday from 7:30 to 7:45 A.M.

The news is written and presented in a fashion designed to be of interest to the elementary school child with strong emphasis on visuals and on pronunciation and spelling of place names and names of people in the news. Carefully edited and narrated film material is used to supplement visual reports. Each day a special study in depth is made of one news item. A simple news set is used: rear projection screen, globe, maps, and blackboard.

A key element in the preparation of JUNIOR NEWS REVIEW is feedback from those who use it. Through liaison with the county school administrators' association, the station is in regular touch with elementary school teachers throughout the county. Periodically the teachers return questionnaires commenting on the program and making specific suggestions on treatment of news and analysis for this age group.

While JUNIOR NEWS REVIEW is directed to enhancing the child's general informational level of what is going on in the world and is not geared to the formal instructional process, teachers do use it as a source of background information for classroom discussion.

The program is fully sponsored.

Expedition Northwest!

Seattle, Washington

EXPEDITION NORTHWEST! communicates a sense of excitement while informing its young viewers about the past and present of the region in which they live. From a day in the life of mountain goats on the Cascade Trail to reminiscences of the great Seattle fire of 1889 by a 95-year-old eyewitness, the programs capture and transmit important elements of life on one of America's last frontiers.

Devoting as much as 250 hours to the writing, preparation, and filming of each half-hour program, the station's special projects unit shoots most of its film on location, but also utilizes film made by amateurs who happened to be on the scene at the time of a significant occurrence. Viewers of EXPEDITION NORTHWEST! have followed rivermen driving their logs 80 miles downstream through the rapids of the Clearwater River in Idaho; they have ridden with an eastern Washington pilot in his crop-duster airplane spraying wheat and apple crops; they have recaptured the spirit of the whaling fleet that sailed out of Vancouver until just a few years ago.

Working in cooperation with the Seattle and King County Public Schools, teachers' study guides and synopses are prepared for each broadcast and distributed throughout the school systems. Audience reports suggest that well-produced documentaries on subjects of high local interest in combination with vigorous publicity and promotion efforts can succeed in attracting and holding sizable audiences at 7:00 P.M. on Mondays.

EXPEDITION NORTHWEST! makes use of the half-hour made available every third week by a network series to explore the wealth of material—historical as well as actual—to be found in the Washington area. In the highly diverse patterns of life through the United States, opportunities exist for relating the child to aspects of his world; many of these he can come to know only through television.

Here's How
Jacksonville, Florida

Not so long ago, it was possible for a child to learn about how things are made by seeing it done at home or in his immediate neighborhood. Bread, pickles, candy, ice cream, butter, and clothing were made at home; horses were shod, tools were repaired, and metal tires were put on wheels at the local blacksmith's. HERE's HOW makes an effort to bridge the widening gap between the child's curiosity ("How do they do that, Daddy?") and the increasing remoteness and mechanization of the manufacturing process.

Several weeks in advance of a scheduled broadcast, the program hostess and a group of three children visit a factory within a 75-mile radius of Jacksonville. They are accompanied by station cameramen who film the visit in detail. After the film has been processed and edited, the program is broadcast with the children providing the narration; they describe how the product is made and what it is used for. A paper plant, a candy manufacturing plant, and a sausage factory have been among the places visited.

A regular five-minute feature of this Saturday morning, half-hour program is a dance by a children's dance group based on the theme of that day's visit. A clown, who is also a ballet teacher, performs an appropriate comedy number.

Every community has its places of interest that children rarely get a chance to see. Television can be very effective when it helps the child learn about the "hows" of the workaday world.

Wifdlife
St. Louis, Missouri

With increasing urbanization, fewer and fewer children (or adults) have a chance to learn about wild animal and plant life under natural conditions. WILDLIFE, a half-hour Saturday afternoon program, aims to inform its viewers about the characteristics and habits of our native wildlife and to draw attention to the role that every good citizen must play in wildlife conservation.

A well-known local artist-naturalist-photographer serves as program host in this series, which takes up one species in each broadcast: eagles, tree squirrels, beavers, black snakes, falcons, spiders, turtles, and wolves are examples.

Viewers first become acquainted with each program's subject through a live specimen, slides, or drawings, or all three in combination. The life pattern of the animal is explained, together with its part in maintaining the balance of nature. Each broadcast usually includes some ten minutes of film dealing with some aspects of the animal's life, its usefulness to man, its place in history.

Studio production is simple. The host works at a picnic table set in front of a rear-screen projection of an outdoor scene appropriate to the particular program and at an easel for drawings and sketches. He is joined by the station's attractive weather girl,who asks the kinds of questions that viewers might ask.

WILDLIFE is produced in cooperation with the St. Louis Public Schools. In addition to normal promotion channels, advance information about the programs in the series is sent to some 750 elementary and secondary schools in the City and County of St. Louis, as well as in contiguous areas of Illinois.

The Magic Tree
Providence, Rhode Island

In a culture that puts great emphasis on youth, where the three-generation household has become increasingly rare, the contribution to a child's education that can be made by the grandparent is often overlooked, if not rejected. The host figure on television programs for children tends to be young—in the tradition of the nursery school or kindergarten teacher—or ageless—in the tradition of the stylized clown. A notable exception is found in THE MAGIC TREE, a late Sunday morning, half-hour program of facts, stories, and artistic impressions, presided over by a grandmotherly hostess with a professional background in fine arts and design, writing, the stage, radio, and animal rescue work.

In a woodland setting stands the magic tree, surrounded by large toadstools, grass mats, a running brook, a "natural" well, and the hostess's treasure chest. A typical program in February began with a prayer and included a winter poem; a recording of "The Skater's Waltz" (skated to by a puppet); a conversation about the week's birthdays (Thomas Edison, Galileo, Abraham Lincoln) ; a filmstrip on Lincoln; and a brief segment on St. Valentine's Day. Other features that appear regularly include the stone of the month, the flower of the month, "Far Away Places" (still photos and music from other countries), science ("Why do stars twinkle?"), and fairy-tale records behind slide sequences.

The New Bedford Whaling Museum, Rhode Island Society for the Prevention of Cruelty to Animals, Roger Williams Park Museum, and the State Department of Agriculture are among the institutions that provide models, exhibits, and authentication.

Albany, New York

EXPEDITION: 13. Series of complete production of ballets, musicals, orchestral concerts, and specially produced films such as a portrait of the Hudson River. Local talent is used and a drama-and-art critic is host. Age: 4 to adult. Every third Monday; half-hour to 1 hour; live/tape/film; 2 cameras; 20 hours rehearsal; 8 to 60 hours writing and preparation. Some shows sponsored.

Albuquerque, New Mexico

BIRDS, BEASTS, AND LITTLE FISHES. Young pet owners and host discuss the care and enjoyment of pets. Each program takes up a single type of pet and explores its personality and idiosyncrasies, books on its care and handling, and the pleasure it gives its owner. Some pets are offered for adoption. County Humane Association and PTA supply talent and material. Age: 10 to 12. Alternate Friday evenings; 30 minutes; live; 2 cameras; half-hour rehearsal; 10 hours writing and preparation.

Birmingham, Alabama

YOUNG PEOPLE'S WORLD. Current news items reported in story form are interspersed with film clips, reading suggestions, or trips to the local zoo. Local students appear frequently to receive safety patrol awards and read school announcements. Age: preschool to 12. Monday through Friday afternoon; 5 minutes; live/tape/film; 2 cameras; 2 hours writing and preparation.

Boise, Idaho

EXPEDITION. Live and filmed-on-location programs take viewers to such expeditions as a wild horse roundup, a geology exploration, a local murder trial (dramatized by high school students), the Kennedy-Nixon debates (re-enacted by 6th graders), and a demonstration of heart surgery. The schools assign the program as homework. Local governmental, civic, educational, and business groups help on production. Age: 6 to 12 (and family). Saturday evening; 30 minutes; live/film; 2 cameras; 10 to 15 hours preparation; 4 to 8 days for location photography. Some programs sponsored.

Boston, Massachusetts

COMMANDER JET'S COMEDY. Space-age developments are explained with aid of slides, models, and films. The principles of Colonel Glenn's orbit, for example, were shown by video tape of the flight and animated films of the operation of retro rocket firing. The control room of a space ship is the setting. Age: preschool to 12. Sunday morning; 30 minutes; live/tape/film; 2 cameras; 2 hours rehearsal; 4 hours writing and preparation. Sponsored.

LET'S LOOK AT THE WORLD. A 5-minute segment of information about different countries of the world in which foreign children (in costumes) demonstrate customs, artifacts, native songs and dances. Educational film supplements live information. International Institute, foreign consulates, and tourist bureaus cooperate. Age: preschool. Tuesday, Thursday, Saturday, Sunday; 5 minutes; live/film; 5 hours preparation for four weekly program segments.

Buffalo, New York

HERITAGE. A program of American history and the development of the Niagara Frontier. Hostess is curator of anthropology at Buffalo Museum of Science where live portions emanate. Encyclopaedia Britannica films are also used. Age: 6 to 12. Alternate Saturday mornings; 30 minutes; live/film; 2 cameras; 1 hour rehearsal; 10 to 12 hours preparation.

NAME THAT HEADLINER. In this quiz game, one team of school children selects a prominent person whom the opposing team tries to identify. Moderator introduces participants and keeps score, and a teacher judges correctness of answers. A prominent educator is interviewed at midpoint. Buffalo Council on World Affairs and local school boards provide material and participants. Age: 10 through high school. Alternate Sunday mornings; 30 minutes; live/tape; 2 cameras; half-hour rehearsal; 3½ hours preparation.

YOUR MUSEUM OF SCIENCE. Curators discuss nature and science exhibits at the Buffalo Museum of Science. Live animals and plants are exhibited. Age: 6 to 12. Saturday morning; 30 minutes; live; 2 cameras; 2½ hours rehearsal; 10 hours writing and preparation.

Burlington, Vermont

CURRENT EVENTS QUIZ. Three schools represented by 7th and 8th graders compete in this quiz program on news developments of the week. The winner returns to the following program to defend possession of his trophy. Competition is sustained through semifinals and finals. State Department of Education helps on production. Age: 12 to 14. Friday afternoon; 30 minutes; live; 2 cameras; no rehearsal; 10 hours writing and preparation. Sponsored.

Champaign, Illinois

TINKER TIME. Varied format of drawing and "tinkering" (making things with crayons, construction paper, etc.), instructions, exhibitions of arts and crafts, interviews, demonstrations of singing and dancing talent, science and adventure films, and book reviews. Art students are occasional guests. Schools in the broadcast area are given advance program information. Local college faculty members advise on production. Age: preschool and up. Monday through Friday morning; 25 minutes; live/film; 2 cameras; no rehearsal; 5 hours writing and preparation.

Chicago, Illinois

JUNIOR NEWSROOM. A daily newscast for young people covering carefully edited local, national, and international news stories. Supplementing reporter's script are illustrative news film, stills, drawings, live demonstrations, and sound effects. Complete weather forecast is also given. Network and station films are used. Age: 5 to 14. Monday through Friday, early morning; 5 minutes; live/film/tape; 2 cameras; 1½ hours rehearsal; 3 hours writing and preparation. Sponsored.

Cincinnati, Ohio

YOUNG PEOPLE'S WORLD. Program of news events supplemented with Encyclopaedia Britannica film clips, station news film, photos, and a blackboard globe. The public library and area publishers cooperate on production. Age: 6 to 15. Monday through Friday afternoon; 5 minutes; live/film; 1 camera; no rehearsal; 2½ hours writing and preparation.

Davenport, Iowa

OUR MAGIC WORLD. Varied format designed to stimulate a child's interest in reading and the world around him. Dramatized episodes in the life of prominent literary and historical figures, science experiments, puppet plays, musical selections, and arts and crafts demonstrations are staged with children taking part. A student frequently announces and narrates the program. The museum director, children's librarian, and school superintendent help on production. Age: preschool to 12. Saturday morning; 30 minutes; live; 2 cameras; 3 hours rehearsal; 5½ hours preparation.

Detroit, Michigan

B'WANA DON. A local pet-shop proprietor shows and discusses live animals, and his chimpanzee performs in skits, rides a bicycle, and plays the piano. An animated animal band and glee club provide musical fun, and cartoons are shown. No studio audience, but mail response has led to an active pen-pal project with African children (a clergyman in Tanganyika is contact). Stylized jungle set has trading post, waterfall, tree house, and glass-faced display unit for animals. Age: preschool to 12. Monday through Saturday morning, 1

25

hour; Sunday morning, 15 minutes; live/film; 2 cameras; half-hour rehearsal; 16 hours writing and preparation. Sponsored.

Durham, North Carolina

THE FUN HOUR. Pioneer exploration in a mountain-lodge setting. Host demonstrates good camping practices and care of young animals. Occasionally departs from theme to explore wonders of space and science. Guest authorities, Encyclopaedia Britannica films, and cartoons are used. State Hall of History, U.S. Weather Bureau, and Boy Scout Council are among sources used. Age: 6 through teens. Monday through Friday afternoon; 1 hour; live/tape/film; 3 cameras; 3 hours preparation. Sponsored.

Fargo, North Dakota

EXPEDITION, RED RIVER VALLEY. Studies of community water resources, civil defense, education, the arts, fairgrounds, the National Guard, and historical sites video-taped on location. A board of educational, religious, and legal representatives helped inaugurate the program. Age: 10 through high school. Saturday evening; 30 minutes; live/tape/film; 2 cameras; 1 hour rehearsal; 5 to 10 hours preparation.

Green Bay, Wisconsin

FOX VALLEY EXPEDITION. A close-up of the community through films (either produced or obtained) of paper manufacture, migrant labor, a religious order, and school curricula. Children take part occasionally as musicians or panelists. Age: 10 through high school. Every third Monday evening; 30 minutes; live/film; 2 cameras; 2 hours rehearsal; 10 to 28 hours preparation.

Houston, Texas

WORLD OF ADVENTURE. Since 1958 Houston Public Schools supervisor of elementary education has presented a weekly half-hour built around informational and instructional films that are relevant as collateral material for elementary school children. Age: 6 to 12. Sunday; half-hour; live/film.

Indianapolis, Indiana

CAP'N STAR. Stories of ships and sailing told with help of maps, pictures, and music. Host, with live monkey on shoulder, discusses oceans, compass, winds, and exploration in a shipboard setting. "Diver Dan" cartoons are also used. Age: 4 to 12. Saturday afternoon; 30 minutes; live/film; 2 cameras; 1½ hours rehearsal; 12 hours writing and preparation. Sponsored.

YOUNG MR. LIBERTY. High school senior, chosen in station talent search, hosts this program of American history. Subjects such as the Declaration of Independence, Life on the Mississippi, and World Wars 1 and 2 are illustrated with films and models of ships, guns, farm implements, etc. Age: 6 to 12. Saturday morning; 30 minutes; live/film; 2 cameras; 3 hours rehearsal; 4½ hours writing and preparation.

Los Angeles, California

EXPEDITION LOS ANGELES. Series of film documentaries on the city's problems and possible solutions. Area schools cooperate on production and use the program guides in social studies classes. Age: 10 through adult. Every third week, evening; 30 minutes; film; 118 hours preparation. Sponsored.

GREAT MOMENTS IN SCIENCE. Physics professor–host each week recreates achievements in life of a great scientist—Archimedes' principle of buoyancy and of the lever; Galileo's law of the pendulum and law of falling bodies; the many discoveries of Huygens; Oersted and the magnetic compass. Tables and laboratory equipment needed for experiment make up the set. Age: 6 to 12. Saturdays, early afternoon; 30 minutes; tape; 2 cameras; 2 hours rehearsal.

SCIENCE AND ITS MAGIC. Local college professor of physics and three young guests from area junior and senior high schools demonstrate some of the wonders of science—the forms of energy, force of gravity, heat and temperature, electricity and magnetism. As experiments progress, host quizzes helpers to make sure they understand physical principles involved. Age: 6 to 12. Sundays, late mornings; 1 hour; tape; 2 cameras; 2 hours rehearsal.

LEARNING '61 AND '62. Series spotlights school activities: Children, singly or in groups, dance, play musical instruments, sing, demonstrate scientific or school projects; guests discuss teacher-training methods, safety education, and other topics of interest to parents of school-agers. Film clips and other visual aids are used to illustrate subject matter. Age: 6 to 12. Saturdays; 30 minutes; tape; 2 cameras; 1 hour rehearsal.

Minneapolis, Minnesota

EXPEDITION MINNESOTA. Video-taped expeditions take viewers to such places as an atomic energy plant, a Nike location, and historic homes to see such activities as a symphony rehearsal and the harvesting of wild rice. Age: 10 through high school. Every third Tuesday evening; 30 minutes; live/tape/film; 2 cameras; 4 hours rehearsal; 16 hours preparation. Sponsored.

Monroe, Louisiana

AMERICAN ADVENTURE. Short films depicting a conservative interpretation of American civic, social, and economic conditions are shown and discussed by panel of students and adults. National Education Program of Harding College, Searcy, Arkansas, produces the films. Advance programs are sent to schools for classroom discussion. Age: 10 through high school. Monday evening; 30 minutes; live/film; 3 cameras; 1 hour rehearsal; 7 hours preparation and writing. Sponsored.

Norfolk, Virginia

LET'S TALK ABOUT. Hand puppets in a puppet stage setting talk about art forms, drawing, and news of interest to children. Educational films ("A Dairy," "Sponges," "The Statue of Liberty," etc.) are also shown. Age: 6 to 9. Monday through Friday morning; 15 minutes; live/film; 2 cameras; 1 hour rehearsal; 2 or more hours writing and preparation. Sponsored.

Omaha, Nebraska

EXPEDITION: MID-AMERICA. Episodes in the history and development of the community are explored through films and visual aids. Educational, historical, and military organizations help on production. Age: preschool to high school. Every third Monday evening; 30 minutes; live/film; 4 cameras; 12 hours rehearsal; 50 hours writing and preparation. Sponsored.

Pittsburgh, Pennsylvania

SAFARI. Guest animals, the kind one might see on an actual safari; interviews with their owners or keepers; and wild animal hunter films from the Encyclopaedia Britannica library are backbone of this program. Six of the 9,500 "Safari Scouts" appear each time to question guests. Contests are held regularly ("Name the wild red fox," and so on); winner receives a sponsor's product as a prize (birdfeeder and birdfeed). Age: 6 to adults. Saturday mornings, 1½ hours; Friday evenings, ½ hour; live/film/tape; 2 cameras; 1 hour rehearsal; 5 to 10 hours writing and preparation. Sponsored.

Providence, Rhode Island

STORYTIME, WITH BETH CHOLLAR. Original flannel-board stories and descriptions of life in other lands are supplemented with films, book reviews, and visits with Audubon Society and wildlife conservation representatives. Age: 6 to 12. Monday through Friday morning; 30 minutes; live; 2 cameras; 1½ hours rehearsal; 3 hours preparation. Sponsored.

Salt Lake City, Utah

TELL-U-NEWS. After brief national and international newscast, several students (appointed reporters by their schools) report on school news and youth group activities. Station presents awards to school and individual for best reporting. Age: 6 to 12. Saturday afternoon; 15 minutes; live; 2 cameras; 2 hours rehearsal; 20 or more hours writing and preparation.

San Francisco, California

PRINCE LIGHTFOOT. A full-blooded Yurok Indian is program host; with dances, songs, stories, sketches, and artifacts he shows what life in an Indian village was like. Age: 6 to 12. Monday evening; 30 minutes; live/film; 2 cameras; 15 minutes rehearsal; 11 hours preparation.

Seattle, Washington

BUTTONS AND HIS BUDDIES. Buttons is a monkey, and his buddies are a guide-naturalist at the zoo and his assistant. Animals are exhibited live or shown in station-produced films. Interest in animals is also fostered in name-the-animal contests and skits such as launching Buttons into orbit. Age: preschool to 12. Wednesday evening; 30 minutes; live/film; 2 cameras; no rehearsal; 8 hours writing and preparation.

QUIZDOWN. Two teams of elementary school students are quizzed on subjects they have studied in class. School administrators and teachers help prepare questions, and winners select a prize for their school. Program is conducted before studio audience. Age: 6 to 12. Saturday afternoon; 30 minutes; live/tape; 2 cameras; 1 hour rehearsal; 10 to 12 hours preparation.

Shreveport, Louisiana

LET'S EXPLORE. Interview program with panel of several children as interrogators. Guests have included the mayor, municipal officers, musicians, and artists. Public schools select participants. Age: 10 to 12. Saturday afternoon; 30 minutes; live/tape; 2 cameras; 2 to 3 hours rehearsal; 4 to 5 hours preparation.

Toledo, Ohio

EXPLORE WITH ME. A university instructor conducts and explains scientific experiments. School science supervisors advise on production, and some schools incorporate the program through required viewing. Age: 10 to 12. Saturday afternoon; 30 minutes; live; 2 cameras; 1 hour rehearsal; 7 hours writing and preparation.

York, Pennsylvania

EXPEDITION LEARNING. Junior college instructors; public school health, physical education, and instrumental music directors; junior high school counselors; the director of the preschool clinic for cerebral palsy; and a state senator describe and illustrate the community's educational problems and opportunities. The school system's radio and television coordinator prepares the program. Age: varies according to particular program. Every third Monday evening; 30 minutes; live; 2 cameras; 6 or more hours preparation.

Youngstown, Ohio

STANLEY'S JUNIOR REPORTER CLUB. A 10-minute segment of an hour-long entertainment program. Best news story submitted during week by a youngster is read; young reporter appears as guest to receive prize. Pictures, film, or video tape of news event are shown. Age: 6 to 18. Fridays; 10 minutes; live; 3 cameras; 1 hour rehearsal; 11¼ hours writing and preparation.

Doing

Television has often been called a window on the world for children. The programs in this section reverse the circumstance; here the television receiver becomes the doorway to the home, bringing in talented persons to engage children in stimulating activity.

Children doing, acquiring new skills: drawing and painting, folk dancing, making stuffed animals, training pets, carving soap, roping calves. Children improving old skills: baseball techniques, posture, spelling. Children displaying their performing talents: dramatic and musical.

Judging from the reports, music might well be one area that could be further explored as broadcasters seek to involve even more the active participation of the young viewer.

Many parents are concerned about the apparent passivity of the child before the television set. Although the child is absorbed in what he sees and hears, adults believe he would be better off playing games or reading books because they feel the child must be active to enjoy things.

In fact, however, the child participates just as actively in what he sees on television as he does in his other pursuits. The programs discussed here are designed to invite creative participation, to stimulate the child's response in physical or mental action. By imitating the action on the screen, the child responds; he finds new channels for his energy, new discoveries about untried talents, a new knowledge about himself.

Television is a natural medium to show skills in the arts and handicrafts. From the many program formats that follow, one can see the range of activities that can be demonstrated. It is wise to lead children to the use of materials readily available in the home. A good presenter of an arts and crafts program will avoid the use of materials not readily available and will aim to make the young viewer a self-starter.

The presenter himself should be competent in the skills he demonstrates. Children are often inspired by the creative activity of adults who have pride in their workmanship. He must therefore be prepared to allow time for the viewer to follow the steps in construction. He must phrase his words to support his actions and let the picture speak as often as possible.

Sports activities on television become exciting when the young viewer can "participate." Too often the adult tries to pull the child up to his own level, taking no thought for the child's desire to play himself. It is not sufficient to place an adult announcer before an audience of children to describe a series of games at a school athletic program. It is not sufficient to believe that the local peewee football team is itself a good enough show for presentation on television. On close examination of such ideas, we begin to recognize that the performance of very young boys trying to imitate the standards of an adult football game will scarcely be good entertainment for anybody. (It is only the overenthusiastic fathers who derive any real satisfaction here.)

In order to show athletic activities or sports that are suitable for children and which in themselves will make good entertainment, the program director should consult with the local physical education teacher or supervisor. The director will find that exciting trends have developed in physical and health education for children. He will find in gymnasiums and playgrounds new games which are at once most important for the development of the child's body and muscles and pleasurable for the children who perform them.

New and exciting material is available on the modern approach to physical education for children. In grades 1 to 6 there is heavy emphasis on the development of basic skills such as walking, running, jumping, throwing, catching, batting, kicking; skills peculiar to games; and those peculiar to rhythmic activities. Since "junior" children are highly individualistic, they are not yet ready for team games. They need the opportunity to exercise their muscles in order to bring about natural body development. They also need simple games which they can imitate and play among themselves.

Cooperation with the school and the recreation directors of the community can result in an outstanding presentation of creative sports activity for children, which the children themselves enjoy and which at the same time will be highly informative for the parents.

Programs on music and dance require careful planning and the maximum time for rehearsal. The director needs time to work out the most attractive camera work for the presentation of a solo performer. Young viewers respond quickly to the artist at work and appreciate his personality. Close-ups of the conductor's meaningful gestures can give a strong accent to the experience of music. Carefully planned movement of cameras can achieve a visual fluidity that will enhance the presentation and give unity to the production. Naturally, the producer must be thoroughly familiar with the music being performed so that he will be able to develop the most attractive form of presentation.

In the case of dance, great care must be taken to relate the close-ups of a solo dancer to the total movement of the group in the studio. Confused or badly planned camera work quickly results in the loss of the visual unity of the dance sequence. Coordination of camera movement and movement of the dancers captures the essential rhythm of the dance and gives the young viewer a chance for vital participation.

Since many of the programs in this group are activity programs, ample time should be allowed for the children appearing in the broadcast to become used to the studio environment. Large groups are difficult to handle, and often the audience is forgotten if the studio group takes up too much of the presenter's attention. Individual children are most attractive in candid shots of their creative activity. The viewing audience identifies most completely with children who are absorbed in their activity—when self-consciousness is reduced to the minimum. As children learn through the experience of "doing," their activity becomes social for all. Their play ranges from sports through crafts to dance and music. We share the deep contentment of their shining eyes "grave with a perfect pleasure."

Stop! Look! and Listen!

Knoxville, Tennessee

Learning to pronounce words properly can be a serious challenge to the very young. The alternating frustration and attainment are an experience common to every child. A child whose mispronunciation of letters has become habitual (substituting the letter *t* for the letter *s,* saying *talt* instead of *salt*) may find it difficult to break the pattern. Such a child is hard to understand; his speech calls attention to him, and subsequent emotional maladjustment is a possible result.

Stop! Look! and Listen! is a Monday-through-Friday quarter-hour program designed to make learning to speak easy for the preliterate child. Each broadcast is short enough to hold the attention of the pre-schoolers and makes a game of the business of proper speech.

The teacher, a speech pathologist, uses a flannel board to demonstrate visual association between pictures and sounds to a group of children in the studio. One day the children study the sound of *t.* The teacher points to a picture of a clock and says, "That's a clock. Sound: **Tick. Tick.** It's not a *d* sound."

The teacher pronounces the *t* sound; the children repeat it. This is followed by a game: a cartoon duck is pulled up by a fishing rod from a fish bowl. Teacher: "Is the *t* sound in this?" Children: "No!" He pulls up a picture of a table. Teacher: "Where is the *t* sound?" Children: "At the beginning!"

Often a number is placed on the board near the sound for the day— a 7 next to *s,* a 3 next to *p* or *m*—indicating to the parent the age at which the child should be expected to pronounce the sound correctly.

While directed to preschool children at home, the program is used in some schools for first-grade students and has been adapted by parents who find that they, too, can become "speech teachers." This type of program can be produced at low cost with a minimum of rehearsal, *provided* the services of a competent speech therapist are available.

Let's Experiment
Milwaukee, Wisconsin

LET'S EXPERIMENT shows children aged 9 to 15 how to do simple scientific experiments that illustrate the fundamental laws of nature and their application. It attempts to build on the natural curiosity of children and their pleasure in exploring and doing things for themselves, which can be heightened during the "middle years" of childhood.

By concentrating on experiments that the children can perform at home, on their own, with materials that are easily come by, it leads them to learn about the world of science and nature by *doing*.

A public school teacher conducts the program from a simulated laboratory in the television studio. Each broadcast deals with a single subject (heat, glassblowing, standards of measurement, centrifugal force, reflexes) and emphasizes the "why" and the "how" as well as the "what." A sense of the dramatic helps attract and focus attention: A program on collecting insects began with the teacher eating fried grasshoppers. The homely is made as attractive as the exotic: how to make toothpaste. And adult concerns are not overlooked: safety in laboratory techniques.

Produced since 1952 with the cooperation of the Milwaukee Public Museum, LET'S EXPERIMENT takes 12 hours of preparation by the teacher and 3 hours by the director for each weekly quarter-hour program, which is broadcast on Saturday afternoons. The Museum makes the teacher available and provides program promotion through bulletins circulated to schools and other educational centers.

By directing itself to what the child himself can do, LET'S EXPERIMENT has helped transform the child's role in learning about science from passivity to eager activity.

Art with Judy
Harrisonburg, Virginia

This half-hour weekly program has a very frank and explicit purpose: to teach youngsters how to draw. It is a straightforward effort, and because its goal is to help those *already* interested, it is presented without extraneous production devices. (Other programs, designed to encourage younger viewers with shorter attention spans to participate in this activity, are described elsewhere. See, for example, Providence, Rhode Island, DRAW PODNER.)

Students (three to five each week) sit at benches with drawing boards in a semicircle. In the center are the teacher at her drawing table and the model. The cameras give home viewers frequent shots of the subject, permitting them to draw along with the studio students. Basic and realistic drawing is taught, with lots of encouragement for beginners. The importance of a preliminary sketch is emphasized. Even professionals, it is pointed out, may make mistakes in a sketch.

Some of the subjects covered are portrait, still life, and landscape (for which the whole program moves outdoors). The station is situated on a hill with a view of the surrounding farms and mountains. Composition, value of shadows, caricature, perspective, the human figure, and foreshortening are also covered. The animals posing "live" have included ponies, sheep, a kangaroo, members of the ape family, and cattle. Human figure study has included the drawing of children and adults. Charcoal, chalk, and watercolors are the media used. Each program is one complete lesson.

The teacher explains the subject for the day, gives instructions, and everybody begins to sketch. When the preliminary sketch is done, the teacher criticizes each student's drawing. When the work is finished, another individual criticism is given.

Viewers are encouraged to send in pictures they have drawn at home. Once a month these are criticized on the air, and the students who appear on the program are chosen from those submitting drawings.

Hop, Skip, and Dance
San Francisco, California

The preschool child shows his love of body movement in many ways: riding a tricycle or hobbyhorse; climbing a jungle gym; running when his more sedate seniors walk. HOP, SKIP, AND DANCE stimulates the use of movement in order to arouse in the child a creative awareness of the world about him.

The program's host, a trained dancer and choreographer, works with eight or ten children in the studio and a pianist (off camera) who improvises a running background accompaniment. The youngsters arrive on set with conspicuous action—tumbling, turning somersaults, or running. They loosen muscles and tension by rhythmic body movements. They say "how do you do" with their shoulders, "it's a nice day" with their hips, and "goodness gracious" with their feet. Children at home, reportedly upwards of 40,000, join in with the studio group.

After the loosening-up period, the host may tell a story—classic, fairy tale, folk tale, or animal fable—and the children dance it out. Or he may talk about the weather with an umbrella and a pair of rubbers, and the children become raindrops and snowflakes. He might bring a basket of kitchen utensils, and the children dance around the floor setting the table, cutting meat, serving ice cream.

A weekly Friday afternoon half-hour program, HOP, SKIP, AND DANCE has been on the air since 1955. The participating children come from regional cooperating nursery schools and dance groups.

4-H Hour
Atlanta, Georgia

The role of 4-H clubs in encouraging farm youngsters to improve their knowledge of agricultural techniques, in stimulating activities beyond those associated with farm routine, and in fostering the ideals of rural America has long been recognized. Since 1955, an Atlanta television station has organized and broadcast a series of weekly half-hour programs in which 4-H members from more than 60 Georgia counties demonstrate their activities and skills.

A typical pre-Christmas program included one girl demonstrating how to make stuffed animals and another showing how to make shuck dolls. A boy gave an exhibition on safety with firearms which was coupled with an industrial film on their use. A third girl performed a piano medley of Christmas carols. The district agent on 4-H programs and the program's producer explained how 4-H members could participate in the Voice of Democracy contest.

Working in cooperation with the state department of agriculture and the University of Georgia's Agricultural Extension Service, the producer of 4-H Hour visits each county in advance to plan each production with the county extension agent and to rehearse the program participants in their demonstrations and performances. The following week, the group goes to Atlanta for further rehearsal and video taping in the studio.

Serving the needs of the farm community in an area where agriculture is a primary activity can be among television's most important functions. Through the availability of existing 4-H organizations, as well as through state and Federal extension services, the pattern of Atlanta's 4-H Hour can be followed elsewhere in providing a special service for the farm child.

Creative Crafts

Oklahoma City, Oklahoma

Imaginative use of existing community resources is often the key to programming that makes a positive contribution to the life of the young viewer. The Oklahoma City Libraries conduct a half-dozen series in their ongoing Community Workshop project. One such project, designed to accommodate the interest of children and their parents in cultural and homecraft arts, has been the basis of a series of weekly half-hour Saturday morning broadcasts since September, 1951.

The subjects and skills taught in CREATIVE CRAFTS include paper sculpture, finger painting, coin collecting, modes of architecture, wall decorations, ceramics, photography, mosaics, Mexican handcrafts, wire-craft miniatures, plastic crafts, picture framing, astronomy, music, and dance.

The instructor for each broadcast—each an expert in his field—may be a teacher from the city schools, the university, or the Science and Art Foundation; a city symphony musician; or a prominent local artist. A hostess, recruited from the library workshop, shepherds the three or four youngsters who appear on each program, working with them as they respond to the instruction of the guest teacher. The set varies depending on the subject, and the props are accommodated to the material being discussed.

Through these broadcasts the television station is able to help extend the usefulness of the workshops from a few hundred participants at the main library to several tens of thousands of viewers in their homes.

Albany, New York

SCIENCE FAIR. Two or three young scientists present and explain their prize-winning experiments, while a guest science teacher supervises. Program produced in cooperation with Niagara Mohawk Council for Educational Television. Schools in northeast area participate and send students. Set includes equipment needed for experiments. Age: 8 to 15. Saturday morning; 30 minutes; tape; 2 cameras; 1 hour rehearsal; 5 hours preparation.

Albuquerque, New Mexico

HABLEMOS ESPANOL. Elementary Spanish conversation instruction by Spanish-speaking public school teacher. Vocabulary reinforcement through objects, pictures, and other visuals; spelling through blackboard work and superimposition of dialogue. Study guides may be purchased. Age: 6 to 9. Monday and Wednesday evening; 30 minutes; live; Tuesday and Thursday morning, tape repeat; 2 cameras; half-hour rehearsal; 2½ hours writing and preparation.

HABLEMOS MAS ESPANOL. Intermediate instruction in Spanish conversation by Spanish-speaking public school teacher. Objects, pictures, and other visuals used to stress vocabulary; blackboard work and superimposition of dialogue to clarify spelling. Study guides may be purchased. Age: 10 to 12. Tuesday and Thursday evening; 30 minutes; live; 2 cameras; quarter-hour rehearsal; 2 hours writing and preparation.

Atlanta, Georgia

MISTER PIX. This is the name of the artist who demonstrates how to draw. "Pixie," a 10-year-old girl, helps. To invite home drawing, children's records are played as Mr. Pix draws cartoons. Children's drawing requests go to "Magic Mailbox"; one is selected each time for on-the-spot drawing. The "selectee" receives the drawing plus a prize. Local theatre, scouts, and others participate. Set contains art props, puppet set, mailbox, etc. Age: preschool to 12. Saturday morning; 1 hour; live/tape; 2 cameras; 1 hour rehearsal; 8 hours preparation. Sponsored.

Boston, Massachusetts

JUNIOR BOWLING. Four teams of five youngsters each are matched by age and skill in a weekly bowling competition under rules of the American Junior Bowling Congress. Program is recorded on video tape at a suburban bowling alley. Age: 8 and up. Saturday afternoon; half-hour; tape remote; 2 hours preparation. Sponsored.

WINNING PINS. Girls and boys compete in bowling matches for money prizes in the form of academic scholarship awards. Two matches are featured weekly: one between two girls, the other between two boys, in the 9 to 15 age group. Winners return the following week to meet new challengers. State Bowling Association determines contestants, supplies uniforms and scholarship money. Age: 6 to 15. Sunday; half-hour; tape; 3 cameras. Sponsored.

Buffalo, New York

FUN TO LEARN. Four members of State University College of Education conduct four late-afternoon instructional series: "French for Children," Monday; "Learn about Books," Tuesday; "Learn about Music," Wednesday; and "Little World Around Us" (nature study), Thursday. Program brochures distributed by station include word lists, songbooks, and reading lists. Age: 6 to 9. Monday through Thursday; quarter-hour; live/film/tape; 2 cameras; 45 minutes rehearsal; 10 to 12 hours preparation.

JESSE KETCHUM AWARDS. An annual program recognizing the scholastic achievements of local grade-school children. Named for an educator and philanthropist, the gold and bronze medals are presented in auditorium setting to an average of 60 children in presence of mayor, superintendent of schools, and Fund president. Highest-award winners, civic and academic leaders give brief talks. Age: 10 to early teens. Sunday afternoon; half-hour; tape; 2 cameras; 1½ hours rehearsal; 13½ hours preparation.

LET'S HAVE A HOBBY. Each week a different boy and girl exhibit and describe their hobbies, explaining how they got started and the satisfactions derived. Local art dealers contribute supplies and services; names of guests are recommended by arts and crafts instructors from area schools. Family game room set includes long table for hobby display. Age: 6 through early teens. Sunday morning; quarter-hour; live; 2 cameras; 1 hour rehearsal; 4 hours preparation.

UNCLE JERRY'S CLUB. Uncle Jerry, program host, conducts a talent program for children before a young audience. Youthful amateurs, who compete for prizes, are judged by their peers in the studio and by home viewers (through mail ballots). Party setting, with gay flats, tablecloths, and hats, is used. Age: 6 to 12. Sunday; half-hour; live; 2 cameras; 2 hours preparation. Sponsored.

Charlotte, North Carolina

INSIDE SPORTS. Techniques and plays of various sports are discussed and demonstrated by high school athletes. Local high school coaches appear as guest instructors. A host coordinates entire production. Set varies according to featured sport. Program in coordination with local coaches' association. Age: 10 through high school. Saturday morning; 30 minutes; live; 2 cameras; half-hour rehearsal; 4 hours preparation.

Columbus, Ohio

FRANZ AND MR. MAGOO. "Magoo" cartoons supplemented with simple experiments and demonstrations of how to make toys, musical instruments, etc., employing household objects. Each finished item must be usable. Setting is Franz' workshop decorated in Bavarian fashion. Age: 6 to 9. Saturday morning; half-hour; live/film; 1 camera; 1½ hours rehearsal; 10 to 12 hours writing and preparation. Sponsored.

TV KINDERGARTEN. Program contains many kindergarten school elements. There are also a celesta player to accompany songs; Franz, a Bavarian toymaker; "Mr. Tree," an animated painting; "Twinkle," a musical voice to announce birthdays. Twice weekly local school children take part in songs, crafts, poems, stories, etc. Hostess is trained schoolteacher. Set has indoor classroom and outdoor garden. Age: preschool. Monday through Friday morning; 25 minutes; live/film; 1 camera; half-hour rehearsal; preparation dependent on hostess.

Dallas, Texas

P. S. REVIEW. Children from fifth and sixth grades deliver prepared comments on daily school activity. Each program features a pupil from different school. With teacher guidance he writes a script on topic which Coordinator of Elementary Education screens. Set shows student at news desk with photo of his school in background. Age: 10 to 12. Every other Tuesday afternoon; 5 minutes; live; 2 cameras; 1 hour rehearsal; 4 hours preparation.

Dayton, Ohio

ADVENTURES IN ART. Simple art projects like drawing and work with construction paper are explained by art teacher to viewers and studio students. Teacher helps students and shows their completed projects. Local ETV foundation produces the program. Age: 6 to 12. Saturday morning; 20 minutes; live; 2 cameras; no rehearsal; 2 hours writing and preparation.

Denver, Colorado

SPELLING BEE. Annual spelldown program. Students from Colorado and Wyoming parochial and public elementary and junior high schools participate. Station director for special projects is host and pronouncer. Local schoolteachers are judges. Produced in cooperation with local morning newspaper. Remote set simulates legislative chambers of capitol building. Age: 10 to 14. Saturday afternoon (early April); 1½ hours; live remote; 2 cameras; 1 hour rehearsal; 16 hours preparation.

Detroit, Michigan

JUNIOR SPORTS CLUB. Members demonstrate physical fitness through exercise idea with participation in gym and sports programs. Guest interviews, group exhibitions, or individual experts in all sports activities are conducted by host and hostess. Age: 10 to 20. Saturday noon; 1 hour; live/film; 2 cameras; 15 minutes rehearsal; 1 hour preparation. Sponsored.

Grand Rapids, Michigan

BUCKAROO RODEO. Working cowboy acts as master of ceremonies and sings. Children in audience are instructed in calf roping, prospecting, bronc riding, etc. Guests present skits. Set has rodeo motif. Variety in program made possible with cooperation of local groups and organizations. Age: preschool to 12. Saturday morning; half-hour; live; 2 cameras; 1 hour rehearsal; 4 hours writing and preparation. Sponsored.

Green Bay, Wisconsin

CHRISTMAS CHORALS. A pre-Christmas series featuring choral groups from area schools, colleges, and churches. Program begins three weeks before Christmas and runs through Christmas Day. Lighting and visual effects reflect mood and content. All ages. Monday through Friday; quarter-hour; live; 2 cameras; 1 hour rehearsal; 1 hour preparation.

Johnstown, Pennsylvania

SCHOOLMASTER'S CALENDAR. Series by pupils of 10 school districts under teacher direction. Themes feature language arts (third graders express selves in words and drawings); current events (fifth graders' panel discussion); science fair (seventh and eighth graders quiz prizewinning junior high panelists). Produced through local ETV association. Age: 6 through high school. Saturday afternoon; half-hour; live/film/slides; 2 cameras; 7 hours rehearsal.

Kalamazoo, Michigan

'TWAS THE NIGHT BEFORE CHRISTMAS. A Christmas special. Narration, with music provided by Kalamazoo Junior Symphony Orchestra; pantomime, by members of Kalamazoo Civic Theater. Balance of program devoted to yuletide music. Indoor holiday setting. Age: preschool through 12. Saturday before Christmas; half-hour; live; 2 cameras; 16 hours rehearsal; 16 hours preparation.

Kansas City, Missouri

CHRISTMAS CARNIVAL. Annual program of traditional Christmas songs, stories, and games, things to make, decorating ideas. Children participate as workers in Santa's North Pole Workshop. Set also includes residential living room. Age: 6 to 9. Monday through Friday afternoon, November through December 25; half-hour; live; 2 cameras; 1 hour rehearsal; 8 hours writing and preparation. Sponsored.

La Crosse, Wisconsin

THE KIDDIES HOUR. An amateur audience participation program during which young children display their talents and are interviewed by host. Age: preschool to 9. Thursday; half-hour; live; 1 camera; half-hour rehearsal; half-hour preparation. Sponsored.

Lincoln, Nebraska

BEAUTINA ROYAL SHOW AND SALE. Children show their dairy heifers for judging and then put them up for on-the-air auction. Program is broadcast from the State Fair Grounds. University of Nebraska Agricultural School, Future Farmers of America, 4-H club, and local cattle breeders help select calves for show and sale. Age: 10 to 16. Annual; Saturday; 2 separate hours; live; 2 cameras; 1 hour rehearsal; 32 hours writing and preparation.

LINCOLN CHIEFS' BASEBALL CLINIC. Midget league baseball group taught fundamentals of game. Some 500 members attended one-time-only program. Instructors were the field managers of the Lincoln Chiefs (Chicago White Sox' farm club) and of the Cedar Rapids Braves (Milwaukee Braves' farm club). Station sports director was host. Age: 8 to 12. Saturday morning; 55 minutes; live remote; 2 cameras; 2 hours rehearsal; 14 hours preparation. Sponsored.

Mobile, Alabama

JUNIOR AUCTION. Clown personality is auctioneer; "money" is coupons from sponsor's product; and articles up for auction are an assortment of toys and games (with bicycles and radios occasionally among the lot). Young "bidders," assembled on bleachers, bid for merchandise. Age: preschool to 14. Saturday; half-hour; live; 2 cameras. Sponsored.

ST. PIUS X SCHOOL CHOIR. A special Christmas program that featured seasonal songs and Gregorian chants. The 32 children participating wore choir robes and appeared on plain set with risers. Age: 10 to 12. Saturday; quarter-hour; live; 1 camera; 1 hour rehearsal; 1 hour preparation.

Monroe, Louisiana

TV SCHOOL HILITES. Student production presented September to June. Station lines up about 36 schools (elementary, junior high, senior high) from Louisiana, Arkansas, and Mississippi. Each school plans program, submits script to station for review and suggestions. Station provides two hostesses to open and close program and to stand by for smooth performance. Set is in accordance with program. Age: 6 through high school. Monday afternoon; half-hour; live; 2 cameras; 3 hours rehearsal; 5 hours preparation.

New York, New York

CHILDREN'S THEATRE. Youngsters in studio participate in games, stories, interviews, dance, and drawing instruction. Scientific experiments demonstrated and discussed. Film used for how-to-make series as well as religious-educational training. Cyclorama background with risers to seat children used on set. Cooperation of local civic organizations, New York Public School System, New York University. Age: 6 to 12. Saturday morning; 1 hour; live/film; 2 cameras; 3 hours rehearsal; 15 hours writing and preparation.

Oklahoma City, Oklahoma

MISS FRAN FROM STORYLAND. Hostess explores creativity in children—encourages them to draw, write poetry, make cardboard animals. Puppets listen, converse, do pantomime. Viewers contribute samples of creative effort, later shown on "Storyboard." Guests take part; birthdays are announced; contests are conducted. Davey and Goliath show weekly. Set has interior storyland house and yard, worktable, storyboard prop, puppet stage. Age: preschool to 9. Monday through Friday morning; 25 minutes; live/film; 2 cameras; 6 to 8 hours writing and preparation. Sponsored.

Peoria, Illinois

BONJOUR AMIS. Sorbonne graduate teaches basics of conversational French. In games, songs, and drawings, puppets act as students. (Set is a French street with puppets heading for French teacher's home. Second set shows typical French furnishings.) Local Junior Leaguers write material, provide puppeteers, help with production. Initial program planned by Board of Education, which still lends support. Two local stations conduct publicity campaign. Age: 6 to 12. Saturday afternoon; half-hour; live; 2 cameras; 3 hours rehearsal; 33 hours writing and preparation.

Pittsburgh, Pennsylvania

JUNIOR CHAMPIONSHIP BOWLING. Area boys aged 8 through 17 pit their bowling skills against each other for weekly trophies and chance at grand prize (season ticket for pro football or other games). A guest spot on each program is reserved for local sports personality or representative of group interested in juvenile activities; he bowls a game with youngsters and is interviewed by host. Age: 6 to 16. Saturday early afternoon; 1 hour; live/tape; 3 cameras; 2 hours rehearsal; 7 hours preparation. Sponsored.

Portland, Maine

YOUTH CAVALCADE. Those who won audition for the program have an opportunity to perform for viewers. They are introduced by a host and hostess. The viewing audience casts its votes for the winner by mailing postcards to the station. Program is in cooperation with the Maine Dairy Council. Age: preschool and up. Monday evening; half-hour; live; 2 cameras; 1½ hours rehearsal; under 3 hours writing and preparation. Sponsored.

Portland, Oregon

SCIENCE IS FUN. Program is part of a regular weekly feature, "Community Workshop." During winter months segment is used by county schools; in summer, by Oregon Museum of Science and Industry. Educational director of museum acts as host about museum activities, demonstrations for home experiment, encourages participation in local field trips. His children, aged 6 and 8, appear as assistants. Age: 10 to 12. October to May, once or twice a month; June to September, weekly; half-hour at noon; live/tape; 2 cameras; 1 hour rehearsal; 4 hours writing and preparation.

Providence, Rhode Island

DRAW PODNER. Unlike the title, this is an art lesson on television presented by a nationally syndicated cartoonist and his schoolteacher daughter. Program includes simple drawing exercises; tricks by Pierre, a French poodle; filmed sequence of cartoonist's visit to a school art class; handicraft lesson. Children sometimes take part to promote Boy Scout week, etc. Set represents artist's studio. Program in cooperation with local schools and civic areas. Age: preschool through 9. Saturday morning; half-hour; live/film; 2 cameras; 2½ hours rehearsal; 6 hours preparation.

Rochester, Minnesota

CHILDREN'S THEATRE. For younger children, a master of ceremonies reads stories; for older ones, the program encourages participation at home through scientific experiments. Some films are shown, e.g., "Light Time," "Davey and Goliath," travelogs, and comedies. Set is typical schoolroom. Age: preschool to 9. Monday through Friday afternoon; 55 minutes; live/film; 2 cameras; 1 hour rehearsal; 1½ hours writing and preparation. Sponsored.

Rochester, New York

KATIE'S HOUSE. Several elements are tied in each week in Katie's living room. Two young guests participate in activities planned by the hostess. They concentrate mainly on ways to have fun on a rainy day, a song guessing game, making paper-bag puppets, acting out a fairy story or Biblical tale, a nature study, or songs accompanied by an autoharp, closing with a brief prayer. Program handled by resource committee of local Presbyterian church. Age: preschool through 10. Saturday morning; half-hour; tape; 2 cameras; half-hour rehearsal; 10 hours preparation.

San Francisco, California

FUN WITH SCIENCE. Science teacher demonstrates experiments that children can set up at home. Host is science coordinator for school district, assisted by station staff member. Set is home science laboratory. Age: 5 to 10. Wednesday afternoon; half-hour; live/film/tape; 2 to 3 cameras; 1 hour rehearsal; 11 to 16 hours preparation. Sponsored.

TIME FOR MUSIC. A music appreciation program led by a hostess who plays the guitar for 12 studio guests. Children learn words and tunes of rounds and folk songs, are introduced to orchestra instruments, make and play percussion instruments. They learn time changes, the melodic shape of tunes, and simple harmony; they are also exposed to improvisation, with emphasis on repetition. Children surround hostess seated on stool. Set has background of two-dimensional "musical carousel." Age: 6 to 9. Monday afternoon; half-hour; live; 3 cameras; half-hour rehearsal; 8 hours writing and preparation.

Springfield, Illinois

KID'S BASEBALL. The pros and cons of Little League baseball, beginning with its origin in 1938, presented by a host-sportscaster. The station filmed interviews, action shots, and live segments showing outstanding sportsmen, coaches, recreation experts. Children appeared in filmed sequences of Little League activities. Set staged with sports montage background. Age: all ages.

One time only, July 7, 1961; half-hour, morning; live/film; 2 cameras; 3 hours rehearsal; 20 hours preparation.

KIM'S KIDDIE KORNER. Drawing talent of hostess is used to instruct and entertain children and to promote public service subjects (bicycle safety, Red Cross foreign package exchange). Children send in pictures they have drawn and also appear as guests to discuss activity of interest to audience or to participate as winners in occasional drawing contests. Cartoons are featured between live segments. Age: preschool to 9. Monday through Friday afternoon; half-hour; live/film; 1 camera; 15 minutes rehearsal; 2 hours preparation. Sponsored.

Terre Haute, Indiana

CHILDREN'S WORLD OF MUSIC. New techniques of gaining music appreciation and participation through freedom of expression were demonstrated on film. Guests were music instructor and elementary school students. Harpsichord and other instruments discussed in relation to French and Mexican cultures under study by students. Program in cooperation with Music Department, Indiana State College. Classroom setting. Age: 6 to 12. Friday afternoon, February 10, 1961; quarter-hour; live/film.

GATEWAY TO CREATIVITY. A special program built around Children's Art Month. Film of classroom art activity supplemented with studio demonstration by 14 students and art professors. Films of student art and exhibits from local art gallery integrated into program. Produced in cooperation with Laboratory School, Indiana State Teachers College, and art chairman of county school. Set had art props and table. Sunday afternoon, March 12, 1961; half-hour; live/film. Sponsored.

THE VOICES OF CHILDREN. A musical special featuring a choral group, minuet dancers, a baroque ensemble, and ballerina from the Music Department of Indiana State Teachers College. Children 6 to 15 years participated. Musical accompaniment of harpsichord, violin, autoharp. Brief explanations and background of song styles, instruments, dances given throughout program by choral director. Age: 6 to 12. March 28, 1961, evening; 30 minutes; live.

Tulsa, Oklahoma

JUNIOR AUCTION. An average of 30 children, seated on bleachers, bid for toys, games, and yard equipment, using coupons and bottle caps from sponsors' products instead of money. Before actual bidding, auctioneer demonstrates prizes. At-home audience participates, and winner claims prize on following week's program. Age: preschool to 12. Saturday; half-hour; live; 2 cameras; 1½ hours rehearsal; 11 hours preparation. Sponsored.

SCHOOL THEATRE. To acquaint viewers with school activities, children and their teachers work out techniques of posture improvement, excerpts of plays and operettas, methods to teach the deaf. Station serves in advisory capacity and handles technical problems. Set includes props necessary to program. Program in cooperation with Tulsa public schools and affiliated groups. Age: 6 through senior high. Sunday morning; 30 minutes; live/tape; 2 cameras; 6½ hours rehearsal; 23 hours preparation.

Winston-Salem, North Carolina

THE BOB GORDON SHOW. Host conducts variety program of sports, hobbies, crafts, tricks, games, instructional techniques. Also features guests, films, cartoons. Children appear as talent and demonstrators. Set is desert scene for open and close, with two "flat" areas. In cooperation with local community radio-television council, city schools, kennel club, and others. Age: 6 to 16. Monday through Friday afternoon; half-hour; live/film; 2 cameras; 4 hours rehearsal; 28 hours writing and preparation. Sponsored.

Storytelling

A well-told story sparks the child's imagination. Sometimes by sound alone, sometimes with added visual elements, and sometimes by dramatic presentation, television tells its stories. In dramatic form, the stories become living fantasies; in narrative form, stirrers of imagination and wonder. Linked to a local library, story programs are prompters of children's reading and creators of interest. Stories have a capacity for exploring feeling, character, and social relations at great length; in doing so they can appeal to all age levels.

The simplest form of this type of program is the storyteller telling a different story on each program. The set is usually simple, sometimes amplified by a few props to lend an element of make-believe. Frequently the program is produced in cooperation with local libraries, which feature the weekly story. The viewers may be invited to volunteer their reactions to the librarian.

In more complex form, the story becomes a springboard for tying together a number of elements on a particular topic. Poetry, art, and music may be woven together to provide children with understanding as well as entertainment. The exciting results that can be achieved when this is done point to new areas of experimentation in an ancient art.

He cometh unto you with a tale which holdeth children from play, and old men from the chimney-corner.

Sir Philip Sidney, *Defense of Poetry*

From a very early age, children love to hear a story told. Adults have a natural opportunity for an intimate relationship with the child. Through the medium of a good story the child finds new avenues of self-discovery. By means of well-written books or well-presented storytelling on television, the child is helped toward a richer social life, wherein he feels secure in himself and comes to have a general desire for security in everyone else as well.

There are many ways to program storytelling. At the outset, the director will certainly ask the help of the local librarian for suitable content for his program. In choosing stories the producer should bear in mind that his is a visual medium. He must do more than have the book read on television. The telling of a story by a narrator is an exciting and stimulating experience in the flow of voice and gesture. We are accustomed to the pleasant sequence of chapters in a well-printed book carefully spotted with interesting illustrations. The television producer must capture the same easy flow in his television presentation.

Careful staging of dramatic episodes from books in order to highlight the story can greatly stimulate the interest of the young viewer in procuring the book from the public library to make a further exploration. Some books in particular lend themselves to puppet presentation, since their elements of fantasy can be captured visually by the medium of puppets more effectively than by live dramatic presentation. In addition, graphic artists themselves are often skillful in representing portions of books as the narrator himself tells the story. There is a flow in graphic design which parallels the easy narrative flow of the reader.

In the presentation of picture books for younger children, it is the responsibility of the producer to remount the sequence of illustrations in order that the turning of pages not interrupt the satisfying visual flow. By cutting up the book and arranging the pictures in such a manner that the camera can range easily from picture to picture, the appeal to eye and ear can be unified completely on the television screen.

When puppets are used for representing stories on television, the producer is sure to attract a wide and fascinated audience of children. Since puppets have such a universal appeal, the producer should study the art of puppetry with an eye to the special requirements of television production. The puppeteer should be skillful either in the making of puppets or at least in selecting puppets which themselves are artistically designed. Very often puppeteers tend to make puppets which are for adults rather than for children. The puppets should be simply designed; they should be highly expressive in form, manipulation, and voicing, in order that they may evoke the most satisfying responses from children. Special care is needed to see that the voicing is not too overwhelming for the visual presentation. Children can enjoy a dramatic story told by means of puppets without the tensions that arise if the drama is too realistic. Strident voicing can so overstimulate the sensibility of the child that the manageable visual impact of the puppet fantasy is lost.

Frequently the scripts of puppet shows call for interplay between the puppets and live human characters. Here the producer must make sure that the children can enjoy a thoroughly satisfying and realistic interaction among these characters. Care should be taken with the design of the set so that there is no wide separation between the human dimension and the dimension of fantasy which is the world of puppets. For example, if the puppet characters are themselves animals, then it is imperative that the human character should have a natural relationship with the puppet animal in his environment. It should be natural for an owl to appear on the branch of a tree within easy gaze and communication of the live character conversing with him.

It is important in the scripts of puppet shows that the story itself should provide a significant experience for the youngster. Very often writers will resort to adult conventions of tension and anxiety when they have run out of the normal and natural play situations that children enjoy. In a program like THE FRIENDLY GIANT the children identify with Rusty the Rooster and Jerome the Giraffe as the Friendly Giant assists them in the participation and the understanding of the story books he reads. The Giant never forgets that it may be difficult for a child to extract a book from a book bag. He never forgets that language itself may be beyond the understanding of a child. Instead of stopping the show to explain, the Giant allows the understanding to come about through the natural question-and-answer process of dialogue. Such considerations show how the writer can use puppets whom children love as a means of scaling down the broad experience of the world, which the child in real life may have difficulty comprehending.

Whatever the mode of presentation, children derive great satisfaction from the involvement in artistic visual sequence. It is easy to rely upon the narrator, "the library lady," or some other personality in order to get the content of the story across. If the television director has confidence in the artistic power of his medium he will choose a presenter who understands children and who knows how to share in their simple patterns of play. The challenge to the author of children's literature and the producer of children's television is well summarized in May Hill Arbuthnot's *Children and Books:*

> . . . it should be remembered that all these mass media of entertainment may stimulate creative activities or lifelong interests. Many older girls have become deeply interested in cooking or sewing by way of televised demonstrations. Ballet programs have pushed little girls into dancing lessons. They may not end as prima ballerinas, but they will grow up to be more graceful and poised young women. The science pictures launch boys' interests in exploration or marine life or perhaps in the wonderful camera work back of the science or news pictures. These may become lifelong interests or even careers. Boys also imitate their favorite sports announcers, for better or for worse. Such imitation generally leads to standards of crisp, clear, incisive diction. What radio and television do to help or harm children depends in part upon how young people use them and what guidance they receive from interested adults, at home and in school. It is going to take ingenuity, wit, and wisdom to see that children develop discriminating judgment in their program choices and to capitalize on the best of what they see and hear as leads into other activities and interests of permanent value.

The Little Playhouse
Toledo, Ohio

Young children instinctively find outlets for their creativity in "play acting." Beyond the sheer pleasure of dramatic play, however, a deeper learning purpose is served as the children experiment with expressions and modes of behavior that they might otherwise not encounter. For a half-hour every Saturday afternoon, THE LITTLE PLAYHOUSE channels this interest for children and enlarges on it by gently leading the child on to an appreciation of art and music.

A group of children aged 7 to 11 join with the program's hostess (called "Stage Manager") in a four-part presentation: (1) a story is told; (2) the children act out the story extemporaneously; (3) they listen to a piece of music or look at a painting related to the story and talk about it; (4) they work on a creative project related to the theme.

In the program on textures, "Princess on a Glass Hill" was read to the children, after which they acted out their version of what they had heard. Selections were played from Beethoven's Symphony No. 3 to illustrate "texture" in music. De Heem's "Still Life" illustrated texture in the subject matter of a painting, and Van Gogh's "Wheat Field," texture in material. The children then made collages with different textures of paper and explained why they had selected each paper.

In encouraging children in creative thinking and self-expression in the arts, THE LITTLE PLAYHOUSE is bound by no rigid curriculum: a story about King Solomon provided the framework for displaying Rouault's portrait, "The King"; the theme of Hawaii led to the hula dance and use of the hands to express symbolic meaning; *Winnie-the-Pooh* led to a discussion of the childhood imagination; a program on clowns was climaxed with the drawing of geometric figures; the story of King Midas moved into a consideration of the relative value of material wealth and natural beauty.

58

Woodrow

Cleveland, Ohio

A distinguishing characteristic of this program is its central feature: a half-hour performance by a children's theatre group of a story adapted from the classic or modern repertory. The setting in which the dramatized stories appear is an ongoing 90-minute Sunday morning series designed to attract and hold young viewers through the personality of the host and the diversity of his offerings.

Among the dramatizations have been adaptations of such stories as *The Adventures of Tom Sawyer, Huckleberry Finn, Snow White and the Seven Dwarfs, The Emperor's New Clothes, Ali Baba and the Forty Thieves, Cheaper by the Dozen,* and *Alice in Wonderland.* When appropriate, the plays are presented in two parts on succeeding weeks. All the performances are supervised by the Cleveland Heights Board of Education, which sponsors the children's theatre company. For a typical play, a total of ten hours is spent by the children in rehearsal, including five hours in the studio.

A talented and personable host (Woodrow the Woodsman) plays the flute, performs magic tricks, maintains a small menagerie, presents cartoons, and carries on a fantasy story line leading to the weekly drama. He performs in costume within an imaginative set that includes a forest, a house, and a cave.

Presented in this framework, the plays probably reach more children than they would as a straight dramatic series. (It is reported that more than 70 per cent of television sets in use at this hour are tuned to WOODROW.)

A related advantage—of compelling importance to those interested in the continuation of meritorious children's programming—derives directly from WOODROW's popularity: By virtue of the attractiveness of this program to advertisers, the station is able to amortize the cost of some 56 man-hours of preparation that go into each weekly broadcast.

The Magic Room

Houston, Texas

The library is not only the memory of mankind, but the world's most exciting stage for action, adventure, and discovery as well. To dramatize this concept for young viewers, THE MAGIC ROOM each week examines an idea, an event, a movement, a man, or an aspect of our culture as they are portrayed through the written word and available to all through the books in our libraries.

Among the themes explored by THE MAGIC ROOM during its first three months have been "A Look at Rural America" (*Let Us Now Praise Famous Men; The People, Yes; Cabins in the Laurel*), "Theodore Roosevelt" (*Boys' Life of Theodore Roosevelt; Theodore Roosevelt's Letters to His Children*), "Heraldry" (*A Book of Armour; Boutell's Heraldry*), "A World to Discover" (*The Discovery of the World; Child's History of the World*), "In the Face of the Storm: Story of Hurricane Carla," and "Mark Twain."

Every program uses a book or several books as its takeoff point, but treatment of individual themes varies with the subject. The program on Theodore Roosevelt used a model of a volcano for the Panama Canal episode; a program on Leonardo da Vinci employed models of his inventions, copies of his paintings, and miniatures of his designs; the set for "The Pilgrims Revisited" contained reconstructions of Plymouth Colony furniture and artifacts; Hurricane Carla was depicted through newsreel film and the reminiscences of the men who covered it.

Two writer-director teams are assigned to the series, working on the programs for alternate weeks. Each half-hour program requires some 80 man-hours of writing, research, preparation, and filming, plus seven hours of studio rehearsal. A four-page brochure that includes a synopsis, glossary, follow-up suggestions, and extensive bibliography is prepared every week; 3,500 copies are distributed through schools and libraries. Scheduled between two popular late Sunday afternoon network programs, THE MAGIC ROOM reaches a good-sized audience of children, parents, and teachers.

The Quiet Man
San Francisco, California

Stories are told in many ways: through reading, puppetry, drama, music, and the dance. Virtually all these media are used by broadcasters in their efforts to bring the ancient art of storytelling to television.

Still another form—relatively unused in this country—is employed in this weekly late afternoon quarter hour: the art of pantomime. The star (and sole performer) of THE QUIET MAN is a teacher of English at the California School for the Deaf who studied pantomime under Marcel Marceau in Paris. Wearing the mime's traditional costume and heavy clown make-up, he "tells" the story against a background of simple drapes. An easel which stands to one side of the set holds a title card that tells the name of the story or asks questions to which the 6- to 9-year-old viewer can respond. The Quiet Man does not speak at all; the only sound is theme music designed to involve the viewer more thoroughly into an otherwise completely visual experience.

Pantomime in short segments holds a number of appeals for children; the action challenges the child's imagination and stretches his capacity for understanding so that he becomes, in a sense, a participant in the story. The rewards of a skillful performance are great.

But the hazards of pantomime can be equally great: Unless performed by a sensitive mime with consummate artistry, it turns into slapstick—and the supply of competent performers is very limited.

Yet so basic and fascinating a form of storytelling is pantomime that the reception of THE QUIET MAN by Bay Area viewers might challenge other broadcasters to seek out such talent in their communities.

Let's Tell a Story
New Orleans, Louisiana

This program serves in a dual role to stimulate interest in books. It engages the interest of the children in books through the age-old appeal of storytelling. Having stimulated this interest, it then encourages reading of these books by making them specially available in the public libraries.

Each week, the story to be told is introduced in pantomime by a character in elf costume. The storyteller is dressed in costume and shown in a setting appropriate to the story: medieval dress for *Rapunzel*, pith helmet and hunting clothes for *The Elephant's Child*, matador outfit for *Ferdinand the Bull*, Pilgrim costume for *Indians for Thanksgiving*.

The stories—selected from a list prepared by the public and parochial school systems—are told in straightforward fashion for children from preschool to nine years of age. This quarter-hour program has been produced in cooperation with the New Orleans section of the National Council of Jewish Women since 1958. Members of the Council write and edit the scripts, make costumes, find props, and select the cast. Prerecorded on tape, each program is broadcast on the originating station Sunday mornings. It is then supplied to the ETV station, where it is repeated late Monday afternoon.

Program promotion includes posters on display at all public libraries, 20,000 LET'S TELL A STORY bookmarks made available to children through the libraries, advertisements in *TV Guide,* and regular on-the-air promotion.

LET'S TELL A STORY provides an example of cooperation between broadcaster and community with the program's value extending far beyond the broadcast itself.

Juvenile Theatre

Lincoln, Nebraska

Two purposes are served by this weekly, one-hour program: Local creative talent in the performing arts is encouraged and used on television, and a course for the training and development of talented youngsters is provided.

In cooperation with local music teachers and a school of dancing, the station holds auditions for children twice a year. Those selected become permanent members of a repertory company which will take part in JUVENILE THEATRE for the following six months. The children range in age to 14 years. Because of the nature of some productions, some preschoolers are included (e.g., bunnies in an Easter program).

Each broadcast is keyed to a theme: Hallowe'en, the circus, salute to the Armed Forces, Latin America, seasons of the year, and holidays, with appropriate sets constructed by station personnel. In song and dance, through music and the spoken word, the spirit and significance of the theme is illuminated.

It is *not* a showcase for amateur talent participating in a juvenile variation of a variety show. With over four hours of studio rehearsal per program and instruction and coaching by the continuing host, the children are, in effect, receiving a course in the theatre which one or two stage performances could not accomplish. A total of 20 man-hours of coaching, production, engineering, and design time contribute to the youngsters' sense of participation in the theatrical world—a world most of them could not normally have entered.

Albuquerque, New Mexico

DONKEY TALES. Hostess reads children's stories to a donkey, illustrated by pictures from the books or drawn by the station art department. Setting has fairy story motif. Junior League members prepare the program. Age: preschool to 9. Monday, Wednesday, and Friday afternoon; 15 minutes; live; 2 cameras; half-hour rehearsal; 3 hours writing and preparation.

Cleveland, Ohio

BARNABY'S SATURDAY PARTY. Two characters play out a story line that takes them to imaginary places. Topics include space travel, episodes from American history, and well-known children's stories. Cartoons and films are spread through the program. Setting is a cottage in an enchanted forest. Age: preschool to 12. Saturday morning; 2 hours; live/film; 2 cameras; 3 hours rehearsal; 36 hours writing and preparation. Sponsored.

Columbus, Ohio

FUN WITH BOOKS. Two children summarize books they have read and answer questions from the moderator. Weekly contest awards a book to viewer who writes the best letter about a favorite book. Junior League sponsors the program; local library assists on production. Age: 6 to 12. Saturday morning; 15 minutes; live; 1 camera; 3 hours rehearsal; 9 hours preparation.

KIDS' STUFF. Host sings nursery rhymes and folk songs and tells stories in a program designed to teach and entertain preschoolers. He tells a different illustrated story each day but repeats the song for the week so that viewers may learn it and join in. Ohio State professors advise on production. Age: preschool. Monday through Friday; 15 minutes; live/tape; 2 cameras; 20 minutes rehearsal; 2 hours writing and preparation.

SANTA CLAUS SHOW. Scheduled daily during the month before Christmas, program features Santa Claus, a snow princess, and a puppet. The trio decorate Christmas tree (with ornaments that have children's names on them), examine toy chest, and read mail. Toy-shop setting has adjoining living room with fireplace, picture window, holiday decorations. Age: preschool to 9. Monday through Friday; 15 minutes; live/film; 2 cameras; 2 hours rehearsal; project initiated five months in advance (July). Sponsored.

Denver, Colorado

THE HOOD OF FORGETFULNESS. An original children's ballet written and choreographed by members of the local theatre and ballet companies.

Dancers ranged in age from 4 to 18 and performed in a papier-mâché forest setting. Age: 4 to 18. One time only, Saturday afternoon; 30 minutes; live/tape; 3 cameras; 3 weeks rehearsal; 4 weeks preparation.

Fairbanks, Alaska

GRADE SCHOOLS IN ACTION. Elementary school children present dramatizations, choral programs, and comedy skits. The children conceive and produce the program (paint murals, assemble props, etc.) under the direction of two teachers. Age: 6 to 12. Tuesday evening; 30 minutes; live; 1 camera; half-hour rehearsal; 6 to 8 hours preparation.

Florence, Alabama

EARLINE IN STORYLAND. A local piano teacher conducts a program of singing, dancing, and story reading. Setting is a fairyland of castles and clouds. Age: preschool. Monday through Friday afternoon; 15 minutes; live; 2 cameras; half-hour rehearsal; 1½ hours preparation.

Green Bay, Wisconsin

THE NIGHT BEFORE CHRISTMAS. A one-time-only program of Christmas stories and songs. First half—secular in mood—included popular Christmas songs and readings of *The Night Before Christmas, The Littlest Angel,* and "Yes, Virginia, there is a Santa Claus," with background music. During religious portion, priest retold story of St. Francis and the first crèche, and the Christmas story from the Bible, with carols and sacred music in background. Appropriate visuals used throughout. Local library and Franciscan fathers assisted in production. Age: all. Morning of December 24; 1 hour; live; 3 cameras; 6 hours rehearsal; 8 hours writing. Sponsored.

Greenville, South Carolina

HOW DO YOU SAY IT? Correct diction and meanings of words are taught by drill and oral reading of poetry. University speech professor leads children's group. Age: 10 to 12. Tuesday morning; 30 minutes; tape; 2 cameras; 15 minutes rehearsal; 1½ hours preparation.

Kansas City, Missouri

CHILDREN'S COMMUNITY THEATRE. Children's plays are staged for television and produced by the city's Children's Community Theatre. Half the plays are original. Each production uses from three to seven original sets. Age: 6 to 12. Four times a year, Sunday afternoon; 1 hour; live/tape; 3 cameras; 17 hours rehearsal.

Los Angeles, California

LOOK AND LISTEN. Readings from children's classics, such as *The Ugly Duckling, The Cat Who Went to Heaven,* and *Peter's Pinto.* Storyteller appears in costume appropriate to theme or period of story; sound effects, props, slides, and setting, all in keeping with narration. Los Angeles Public Library cooperates in preparation. Age: preschool to 12. Saturdays; 30 minutes at various times (afternoon); tape; 2 cameras; 2 hours rehearsal; 40 hours preparation.

Milwaukee, Wisconsin

YOUNG MODERNS TALK BOOKS. Young people act out episodes from a favorite book in this program designed to encourage reading. A professional actor narrates the plot between the dramatized sections, then the children and a librarian discuss the book. Public library provides talent. Age: 9 to 14. Saturday afternoon; 15 minutes; live; 2 cameras; 4½ hours rehearsal; 26 hours writing and preparation.

YOUR LIBRARY STORY. Children's librarians read stories from the library collection and display illustrations specially prepared for each story. Public library provides storytellers and materials. Age: preschool. Saturday morning; 15 minutes; live; 2 cameras; 2 hours rehearsal; 11½ hours writing and preparation.

Minneapolis–St. Paul, Minnesota

CHIMNEY CORNER. Children's librarian reads stories and chats with two puppets—a mouse in a bookcase-mousehole and a cuckoo in a cuckoo clock. Setting is a playroom. Age: preschool to 9. Tuesday and Thursday afternoon; 15 minutes; live/tape; 2 cameras; half-hour rehearsal; 11 hours writing and preparation.

Mobile, Alabama

THE PIXIE PLAYERS. A two-part program presented on successive Sundays. The first part, presented in French by a group of preschool children, consisted of a puppet show (*Little Red Riding Hood*), French conversation, and French folk songs. Second Sunday program featured junior high school group in operetta version of fairy tale (*Twelve Dancing Princesses*). The Players made their own puppets, built their own set. French teacher and woman experienced in children's theatre were associated in production. Age: preschool through junior high. Two Sundays in October; 30 minutes; live; 2 cameras; 3 to 4 hours rehearsal; extensive preparation.

New York, New York

LIBRARY LIONS. News items about books available in the city libraries and live and recorded concerts for children are interspersed with informational films. Public library prepares live portions. Age: 10 to 12. Sunday morning; 30 minutes; live/film; 11½ hours preparation.

Omaha, Nebraska

CHRISTMAS IN COUNCIL BLUFFS. A narrator reads the story of the Nativity, children's choir sings Christmas songs, and youngsters reenact the manger scene in this annual Christmas program. Presbyterian Church cooperates on production. Age: preschool to high school. Annual, weekend afternoon; 30 minutes; live; 2 cameras; 6 hours rehearsal; 9 hours writing and preparation. Sponsored.

Philadelphia, Pennsylvania

LEE DEXTER SHOW. Children follow the continuing adventures of an assortment of puppets which alternate with cartoons. Occasionally puppeteer models clay characters or shows how he creates his puppet personalities. Age: preschool to 9. Monday through Friday, 30 minutes; Sunday mornings, 1 hour; live/tape; 2 cameras; 1 hour rehearsal; 2 hours preparation.

Sacramento, California

GOLD RUSH DAYS. Old Man Mountain (a papier-mâché mountain with movable mouth) narrates the adventures that befell one Grizzly Coot in the California of 1849. An artist illustrates the events on camera. Age: 6 to 12. Sunday morning; 15 minutes; tape; 2 cameras; 1 hour rehearsal; 15 hours preparation.

St. Joseph, Missouri

STORY TIME. Librarian reads fairy stories and classic and adventure stories, and hostess-assistant supplements them with related anecdotes and close-ups of story illustrations. On alternate programs, Junior League members dramatize one-act children's plays. Age: preschool to 9. Monday afternoon; 15 minutes; live; 2 cameras; 1 hour rehearsal; 5½ hours preparation.

Salt Lake City, Utah

SANTA CLAUS TIME. During the month before Christmas, Santa Claus reads Christmas poems and stories in a fireplace setting, tells about Christmas customs in other lands in an office setting, and talks with guest children from a throne. Seasonal cartoons are also shown. Age: preschool to 12. Monday through Friday afternoon, December 1–23; 30 minutes; live/film; 2 cameras; 30 minutes rehearsal; 5 hours preparation. Sponsored.

San Francisco, California

STORY HOUR. Storyteller in a cottage setting with fireplace and rocking chair reads tales from folklore, mythology, and the classics. He sets the background for each story and then encourages viewers to seek out the story and related material in the library. Age: 6 to 12. Wednesday afternoon; 15 minutes; live; 2 cameras; 3 hours preparation.

THE POETRY PATCH. A teacher reads limericks, poems, and narrative poetry—ranging from T. S. Eliot's "Practical Cats" to the *Pied Piper of Hamelin*—in a simple setting decorated with floor-standing black cutouts. Age: 6 to 9. Wednesday afternoon; 15 minutes; live/film; 2 cameras; 1 hour rehearsal; 18 to 22 hours preparation.

Seattle, Washington

TELAVENTURE TALES. Six children join the Story Lady and her puppet assistant to talk about the works of a particular author or books on a particular subject (such as family life or dogs). Only books that are in plentiful supply in the library are discussed. Program is produced alternately in Seattle and Portland and city librarians select books and participants. Age: 8 to 12. Saturday morning; 30 minutes; live/tape; 2 cameras; 1 hour rehearsal; 10 or more hours writing and preparation.

Shreveport, Louisiana

CHANNEL 12 SHOWCASE. Dramatization of play, "King Woodenhead's Crown," written for and performed by children and produced by the city's Children's Theatre. Fanciful settings represented a castle and forest. Age: preschool to 9. One time, Saturday afternoon; 1 hour; live/tape; 4 hours rehearsal.

Spokane, Washington

SPOKANE CHILDREN'S THEATER. Television adaptation of the five stage plays offered each season by the Spokane Children's Theater, Inc. Series includes full-length versions of such stories as *Alice in Wonderland, Hansel and Gretel, The Plain Princess, Puss in Boots, The Wizard of Oz*. Sets reproduce stage scenes; children appear as actors or as spectators on camera for prologue or epilogue. Age: 6 to 12. Five times a season; 1½ hours; live; 3 cameras; 3 hours rehearsal.

Syracuse, New York

JACK JINGLES. Puppet dramatizations of famous children's stories and of original stories written by Junior League members. Presented as regular segment of a morning women's program, offering is created and acted by Junior League members. Age: preschool. Fridays; 15 minutes; live; 2 cameras; ½ hour rehearsal; 6 hours writing and preparation.

Terre Haute, Indiana

THE CHILDREN'S ROOM. The Story Lady, a children's librarian, tells stories, talks with preschool guests, and organizes simple games for them to play. Librarians and Sunday school superintendents select participants. Age: preschool. Saturday morning; 15 minutes; live; 1 camera; 11 hours writing and preparation.

Tulsa, Oklahoma

LEWIS MEYER'S BOOKSHELF. On a 5-minute children's segment of this adult program, host reviews children's books. Young guests appear to read from and discuss favorite books. Age: preschool to 9. Sunday morning; 30 minutes; live/tape; 2 cameras; 1½ hours rehearsal; 16½ hours preparation.

Orientation

Programs dealing with school preparation, Bible stories, ethical values, accident prevention, and dental hygiene all have a common purpose: orienting the child to the world, what he can expect from it, and what is expected of him in turn. In one way these programs attempt to familiarize children with coming events and experiences; in another, to inform them as to how they should behave. Many are concerned with manners and morals, prescribed ways of acting in given situations.

Added to and integrated with the sum total of a child's experiences in home, school, and church, television programming can be a reinforcing agent in the process of adjustment. The programs described in the following pages set out to support the family, to assist education, and to give the pulpit a wider range.

*I shall detain you no longer in the demonstration of
what we should not do, but straight conduct ye to a
hillside, where I will point ye out the right path of
virtuous and noble education; laborious indeed at
the first ascent, but else so smooth, so green, so
full of goodly prospect and melodious sound on every
side that the harp of Orpheus was not more charming.*

Milton, *Tractate of Education*

Everyone is familiar with the fear that new ideas or a new technology may have an unsettling effect on children and young people. We are also familiar with the generally conservative character of intellectual and cultural leaders who seem to be reluctant to take up the early challenge presented by new media of communication. Both parents and professional leaders have a mutual concern for the moral and cultural integrity of children and therefore tend to fear the unknown powers of the new media. The same fears and criticisms were expressed at the advent of printing, the penny newspaper, motion pictures, radio, and now television.

Many of these criticisms were without real foundation, with the result that our society has made scapegoats of some media while over-committing itself to traditional institutions. As many parents have come to feel inadequate to provide sound training for their children, they have tended to shift responsibility to the school, the church, and the community. Many programmers, recognizing this shift in attitude, have turned to the church, the school, the service club, and the welfare leader for program content. Unfortunately, programs in this category tend to be moralistic, instructional, and abstract in conception. Too often the producer depends upon the idea rather than the artistic conception of a show which children can understand.

Many children's programs fail because of this emphasis on abstract ideas. Children naturally enjoy specific information and specific action experiences. Their interest reaches a low ebb when the presenter depends upon communication by means of abstractions. We are further reminded that example prevails more than precept. Instead of using direct instruction, the writer or performer might try more indirect methods which will help children to solve problems for themselves. Pictorial demonstrations of how accidents occur with fire or water orient the child to the problem presented and enable him to develop a feeling of personal responsibility for the prevention of accidents.

Since most television is viewed informally under conditions where direct instruction is not possible, the producer will be most effective if he seeks to stimulate the young viewer to creative thinking and action. The use of dramatic presentation by actors or puppets can make issues very real for children. They identify themselves with the characters in the situation and realize the solutions for themselves. If religious programming is worth doing for children, then it should be done in a manner most suitable for the television medium and in a manner consistent with the average child's normal habits of viewing. Such programming should contribute to the child's growth and development into a mature, creative adult. Such programs should make a faith meaningful for a child as he lives his life from day to day. We must always remember that if children do not enjoy a program they will not accept what we as adults provide. Writing about children and books, Paul Hazard makes an observation which has a good warning for the television producer in the selection of program content and personalities for presentation.

> Children defend themselves, I tell you. They manifest at first a degree of inertia that resists the liveliest attacks; finally they take the offensive and expel their false friends from a domain in which they wish to remain rulers. Nothing is done to create a common opinion among them and yet that opinion exists. They would be wholly incapable of defining the faults that displease them; but they cannot be made to believe that a book which displeases them should please them.
>
> Whatever their differences may be as to age, sex, or social position, they detest with common accord disguised sermons, hypocritical lessons, irreproachable little boys and girls who behave with more docility than their dolls. It is as though . . . they brought into the world with them a spontaneous hatred of the insincere and the false. The adults insist, the children pretend to yield, and do not yield. We overpower them; they rise up again. Thus does the struggle continue, in which the weaker will triumph.

Plato's censorship of the poets of Ancient Greece was rooted in his conviction that any force which might hinder the growth of the individual human soul toward maturity was an evil force. There are many varied opinions about "the right path of a virtuous and noble education." The planning of "orientation" programs for the realization of worthy aims in social, moral, or religious education is laborious just because the maximum creative endeavor is required. "Institutional" programs that are moralistic and abstract will likely be unattractive to children. When the presentation is imaginative, the young viewer can experience truth and beauty for himself. By interaction with mature and understanding adults, the child shares in the education of the search for truth discovering the limits of conduct and the proper range of personal freedom. This condition is the goal of Milton's ascent, "so full of goodly prospect and melodious sound on every side that the harp of Orpheus was not more charming." The blend of truth and beauty must be such that the young viewer can enjoy it with the same deep satisfaction he has in his affection for adults whom he trusts. He must find the same joy that he has in games he plays with his young friends. And always the experience of viewing television should open the mind to new sights of beauty and to deeper understanding of himself and his friends.

Treetop House
Chicago, Illinois

Encouraging preschool children to apply what they learn about the world around them is the underlying principle of TREETOP HOUSE, a morning half-hour program broadcast Monday through Friday. When a natural phenomenon such as gravity is explained, the child is shown how to make a toy or play a game that illustrates gravity. The children are encouraged to perform the act as the explanation is repeated, and designs for simple cardboard and construction paper toys are mailed to parents requesting them.

TREETOP HOUSE is presided over by an attractive mother of three with a background in theatre and journalism. She is joined by four children, a marionette, and hand puppets in a set containing two basic elements. The exterior consists of a garden with a stone wall, a pool, a tree trunk, and winding stairs leading up to the tree house; the interior set is furnished as a well-equipped nursery school.

Each broadcast has a central theme, which is presented in terms and concepts attuned to the preschool child: flight, manners, gravity, values in reading and writing, hand puppetry, science experiments (sometimes as basic as showing that paste must be dry before it will hold). Where appropriate, three to five minutes of motion picture film from educational film libraries is used, specially edited and with voiced-over commentary by the TREETOP HOUSE hostess. The guest children respond to questions about what they have seen, and—with the help of hand puppets—act out stories designed to illustrate common social situations.

The underlying motif of the program, expressed by the producer-writer: "Seeing is better than hearing about it; touching it is better than seeing it; and doing it yourself is better than anything." Educational guidance is provided by a staff member of the children's school at the National College of Education in Evanston, and educators from the Chicago Board of Education appear in five-minute segments once a week to help prepare the child at home for school attendance.

TV Kindergarten
Albuquerque, New Mexico

In a community where three cultures and languages—English, Spanish, and Indian—are intermingled, this preschool program serves a unique function. Since all three cultures are being integrated into the public school system and since there are no regular public school kindergartens in the state, this program fills an important need.

TV KINDERGARTEN achieves its objectives by having its teacher-hostess work directly to the home viewer. No children appear on the program; the entire emphasis of each broadcast is to enlist the attention and participation of the preschooler at home.

The content of the program is designed to prepare the child for the first grade through advancing his social, language, rhythm, and motor development, and introducing him to simple arithmetic.

A typical program opens with the teacher at the piano, the salute to the flag, and a review of materials needed (identified in the previous broadcast). Plants and flowers are examined and a garden is planted with the teacher demonstrating soil preparation, planting, watering the soil, and other aspects of cultivation. Creative movement and self-expression are encouraged: the children pretend they are plants. A short rhythm demonstration follows, and the program closes with an announcement of materials needed for the next day and a reminder to care for the just-planted garden.

Guided by a special committee of representatives from the State Department of Education, the Albuquerque public schools, and the University of New Mexico, TV KINDERGARTEN is broadcast live, twice daily (morning session, afternoon session), Monday through Friday.

Tottle
Philadelphia, Pennsylvania

In this weekly half-hour series for children from 4 to 10, the adventures of a puppet family, the Tottles, serve as the framework for learning how to cope with life's problems in a sound, emotionally healthy way.

The adventures of Mother, Father, Taffy, and Coslo Tottle—and their friends—reflect the normal problems that an ordinary family must deal with on a day-to-day basis. The continuing set of characters, having the fantasy appeal of puppets, help lead the child viewer into a well-balanced adjustment with his social environment, without seeming to preach, patronize, or condescend.

For example, one program was based on Coslo's attempt to keep his parents from finding out about his having misbehaved in school. He intercepted and destroyed a letter from the school, which turned out to be a request for permission for Coslo to try out for the football team. Coslo learns that his own lying and attempt to cover up resulted in his being kept off the team.

TOTTLE also employs the dimension of a play within a play. One of the favorite parlor games in the Tottle household is puppetry. The Tottle children have their own miniature puppets, which they use to tell stories that illustrate a point or, in good therapeutic fashion, to act out their aggressions. Thus, in a program that had selfishness as its theme, Coslo Tottle and his sister acted out—through their puppets—the story of King Midas. Coslo was able to make the connection between his greed for playthings and King Midas's greed for gold.

A writer, two puppeteers, a producer, and a director each spend ten hours with every broadcast; the set designer, six hours. A consulting psychologist who supervises each script for content devotes about five hours to each program. Each sequence requires six hours of rehearsal, three of which are in the studio. Three television cameras are normally used, and the entire series is recorded on tape.

What's the Big Idea?

Albany, New York

A child develops his ethical standards and learns to make value judgments in a variety of ways: from the precepts of his elders at home, school, and church; from the examples offered by his family and peer group; from the climate of the times as exemplified by the degree of public morality demonstrated by political and business leaders. Yet, believing that the ethical foundations of behavior should be examined and not taken for granted, the producers of this program for two years presented a weekly half-hour series in which a group of elementary school children from varying socioeconomic backgrounds joined with a clergyman in discussing a specific situation that raises basic ethical and moral issues for children.

Each broadcast began with a brief dramatization of a problem that the youngster is often called upon to face as he adjusts to life in an adult world: How do you react if you don't get the Christmas gifts you were hoping for? Is there a difference between raiding the cookie jar at home and stealing a comic book from the corner store? Do you admire your father if he goes through a red light and gloats over it? How do you feel about a grown-up who dodges paying his full income tax?

Following the dramatic skit, the children discussed the question under the minister's guidance, in an attempt to reach a consensus and to express varying points of view. Problems to be discussed were frequently based on suggestions contained in audience mail.

The universality of this program concept suggests its applicability in many communities. Broadcasters will recognize, however, that a primary factor in the success of such a program lies in the skill and sensitivity of the moderator.

The Friendship Show

Chicago, Illinois

Today it is generally recognized that *tolerance* is no longer enough; the conditions of life in metropolitan areas increasingly require the mature person to recognize that heterogeneity of ethnic and cultural background can make a positive contribution to the community. Since 1957, THE FRIENDSHIP SHOW has sought to use a weekly, half-hour television program to foster such recognition among children through shared play and learning experiences.

Youngsters from settlement houses and orphanages, from Asian, Central American, African, and European backgrounds, raised in the Protestant, Catholic, Jewish, and Buddhist traditions, all come to THE FRIENDSHIP SHOW. They dance and sing songs of foreign lands, they practice drawing, become familiar with the habits and care of live animals, listen to stories, make up games, act in skits. Participating together without self-consciousness, the children themselves provide a lesson that cannot be lost on those viewing at home.

Educational guidance is provided through a consultancy relationship with DePaul University and a curriculum consultant to the Chicago Board of Education. Resource material and personnel come from the Museum of Natural History, the Art Institute, Museum of Science and Industry, Adler Planetarium, and Chicago Zoological Society.

Kindergarten College
Indianapolis, Indiana

A number of distinct patterns appear in the orientation programs that have been developed for preschool children. One typical format makes use of one character only, the teacher or hostess. Another adds puppets. A third brings in other people, in their real-life roles, who make a substantive contribution. KINDERGARTEN COLLEGE makes use of all these approaches and has added costumed characters from the fantasy world. The resulting combination is a popular one-hour, 9:00 A.M., Monday through Friday program, reported to be viewed by some 75,000 children.

The headmistress of KINDERGARTEN COLLEGE presides over a two-set "campus": a learning area and a play area. Four youngsters each week (selected from people writing in) take part. The hostess leads them in crayon work, and alphabet and number games. The Library Lady, who visits twice weekly, reads stories; a local camp director shows the children some of the secrets of nature; a pet-shop owner demonstrates pet care; a YWCA instructor leads the children in exercises.

Among the fantasy characters are puppets: Jibber (a mouse) and Humphrey Hamstitch (a worm), who engage in badinage; Mr. Copycat (a costumed interpretive dancer), who leads the children in dance exercises; and Phil the Phonograph (a costumed actor), who provides a lesson in music appreciation. These parts are played by members of the stage crew, all of whom participate in local theatrical groups. The producers believe that no small part of the attractiveness of this program to the children stems from the popularity of these fantasy characters.

The informational parts of the program derive from the Indianapolis Public Schools' *Curriculum for Kindergarten Teachers*. Program content is coordinated with the school system's radio-television consultant, the state police (for safety instruction), public library, and YWCA.

Come Little Children
Enter His Gates
Faith of Israel
Philadelphia, Pennsylvania

While the roles of television in religion and of religion in television have still to be clearly defined, many stations have undertaken—in collaboration with church authorities—to program what can be described as "Sunday Schools of the Air." In regions where the population is relatively homogeneous, the church group most representative of the area normally provides the programming leadership. But in large metropolitan centers, broadcasters seek the assistance of all major faiths on a cooperative basis. In Philadelphia, this is achieved in three series of programs presented in rotating 13-week cycles through the cooperation of the Roman Catholic Archdiocese of Philadelphia, the Philadelphia Council of Churches, and the Philadelphia Board of Rabbis.

COME LITTLE CHILDREN offers instruction by a teaching nun in religious themes such as the Life of Christ, the Commandments, and the lives of the saints. A group of seven or eight children participate in the program with the nun through singing and recitation.

The Protestant cycle, ENTER HIS GATES, features Sunday school teachers instructing children in religious stories from the Bible. Music is provided by children's choirs from various churches in and around Philadelphia.

FAITH OF ISRAEL presents Hebrew school and Sunday school teachers who provide instruction in the customs, rites, and history of Judaism. In 1961 a two-part presentation of the Bar Mitzvah ceremony was broadcast on successive Sundays.

The programs are presented on video tape from 11:00 to 11:30 every Sunday morning. Program promotion is provided through on-the-air announcements and news releases on the subject matter of coming programs to local newspapers, magazines, and religious publications.

Baltimore, Maryland *

ROMPER ROOM. Originated in Baltimore in 1953, this program simulates a kindergarten for preschool children, with pledge of allegiance, prayer, physical fitness exercises, weather report, reading readiness, and safety instruction, games, songs, stories, and training in good manners and social adjustment. Approximately six children appear on the program with the ROMPER ROOM teacher for a period of two weeks each. A cartoon may be shown during "rest period." The program format is now syndicated to many cities throughout the United States and Canada. At each television station, the program is conducted with local children and a teacher who has spent at least one week in training in Baltimore. Periodically a representative of "headquarters" visits subscribing stations to assure adherence to prescribed production patterns and standards of acceptable advertising. The format permits sufficient flexibility to cope with local conditions; many variations are found. Both Romper Room, Inc., and stations cooperate with medical and dental societies, the March of Dimes, American Red Cross, the President's Council on Youth Fitness, fire prevention and safety organizations. Age: preschool. Usually Monday through Friday morning; half-hour, 45 minutes, or one hour; live/film; 2 to 3 cameras; 3 to 10 hours preparation. Usually sponsored.

* Local productions also reported from Mobile, Alabama; Phoenix, Arizona; Fresno and Los Angeles, California; New Britain, Connecticut; Orlando, Florida; Boise and Idaho Falls, Idaho; South Bend, Indiana; Des Moines, Iowa; Baton Rouge, New Orleans, and Shreveport, Louisiana; Portland, Maine; Boston, Massachusetts; Grand Rapids, Michigan; Minneapolis, Minnesota; Jackson, Mississippi; Great Falls, Montana; Binghamton, Buffalo, and New York, New York; Cleveland, Columbus, and Youngstown, Ohio; Johnstown and Pittsburgh, Pennsylvania; Providence, Rhode Island; San Angelo, Texas; Salt Lake City, Utah; Richmond, Virginia; Wheeling, West Virginia; Green Bay, Wisconsin.

Buffalo, New York

GOD IN OUR HOME. Catholic clergyman-moderator opens this religious education program with brief explanation of a point of doctrine. He and three young participants from local parochial school discuss problems relating to it. When a good point is made, the moderator draws a line on an easel; object: to draw a perfect house before program ends. Diocese of Buffalo prepares program and arranges children's appearances. Age: preschool to 12. Sunday morning; 15 minutes; tape; 2 cameras; 3 hours preparation.

Chicago, Illinois

SAFARI. Weekly expedition to a foreign country. Host shows film clips of the country, its dances and rituals, talks with native children about their art and customs, and relates facts about their country to religious concepts the viewers can practice. Setting is a world traveler's study. Program is produced in cooperation with the Church Federation of Greater Chicago. Age: 6 to 12. Sunday morning; 30 minutes; live/film; 2 cameras; 4 hours rehearsal; 25 hours preparation.

Cincinnati, Ohio

SIGNAL THREE. Children from studio audience are contestants in safety quiz. Questions relate to traffic, home, fire, water, hunting, etc. Set has wide table to set up a traffic situation. Representatives from local civic, youth, and safety organizations are interviewed. An occasional live remote shows safety practices. Host is safety education director of Cincinnati Police Department, which cooperates on production. Age: 6 to 12. Saturday morning; 30 minutes; live; 2 cameras. Sponsored.

Columbus, Georgia

MISS PATSY'S PLAYHOUSE. Hostess leads young studio guests in games, songs, educational projects, and make-believe trips. Films, cartoons, pictures, and puppets add variety. Nurses, doctors, engineers, firemen, and a pet-shop owner with animal in tow are frequent guests. Program includes a "Mothers' Corner" feature with interviews and hints for Mom. Health, Police, and Fire Departments and public service groups provide guests. Age: preschool. Monday through Friday morning; 1 hour; live/film; 2 cameras; 2½ hours rehearsal; 2 hours writing and preparation. Sponsored.

Columbus, Ohio

HERE'S GRUBBY. Comedy situation program built around television characters. Basic set is a janitor's room in a television station, and the story line is designed to teach a lesson in living. University faculty members frequently assist in production. Age: 10 to 12. Monday through Friday afternoon; 15 minutes; live; 2 cameras; 1½ hours rehearsal; 7 hours preparation.

WONDERBOX. A group of children gather around the moderator—one of a rotating group of local Sunday school teachers—to hear a Bible story, answer questions on religious subjects, sing hymns, and work on projects. Columbus Area Council of Churches furnishes talent. Age: 5 to 9. Sunday morning; 30 minutes; live; 1 camera; 3 hours rehearsal; 9 hours preparation.

Fairbanks, Alaska

SCHOOL FOR FUN. A program of stories, music, toys, and personal hygiene. Teacher-hostess plans lessons in advance for 39-week series and correlates them with material used by local kindergarten and first-grade teachers. Children appear occasionally as guests or to receive awards. Age: preschool. Monday through Friday afternoon; half-hour; live; 1 camera. Sponsored.

Honolulu, Hawaii

THE S.S. ADVENTURE. A Bible quiz in three parts: (1) a series of questions on a chapter of the Old or New Testament; (2) "Who am I?" with clues on identity of biblical personality: (3) a "thought" question for which each team prepares a written answer that is read by one of the panelists. Teams are made up of children from two different Sunday schools. Two films and selection by local choir are presented between quiz segments. Local Council of Churches produces program. 10 hours rehearsal; 22 hours writing and preparation.

Huntington, West Virginia

FUN SCHOOL. Cartoons are interspersed with little lessons (such as five brushes necessary for cleanliness and grooming) illustrated by camera cards, drawings, and narration. The T-Twins—Saf-T, who is always right, and Smart-T, who is always in trouble—give hostess an opportunity to teach good behavior. Sets represent a school interior and exterior. Board of Education and nursery schools helped originate the program. Age: preschool. Monday through Friday morning; 1 hour; tape; 2 cameras; 2 hours rehearsal; 8 hours preparation. Sponsored.

Jackson, Mississippi

DENTAL PROGRAM. Annual program, designed to lessen fear of the dentist's chair, demonstrates dental office equipment, describes new methods dentists use, and explains the results of oral hygiene. Children appear on the program, and a short informational film is shown. Jackson Dental Association cooperates on production. Age: preschool to teens. Annual; half-hour (day and time vary); live/film; 2 cameras; 1 hour rehearsal, 2½ hours preparation.

FIRE PREVENTION. Annual program designed to make youngsters more fire-safety conscious when using matches, electrical appliances, and other items in the home. Shown during Fire Prevention Week with the Fire Chief, City Commissioner for the Fire Department, and children taking part. A short informational film and local entertainment are included. Age: preschool to teens. Annual (day, time, and length vary); live/film; 1 hour rehearsal; 2½ hours writing and preparation.

HOME SAFETY. An annual program produced in cooperation with the Police Department and aimed at making a child safety-conscious. Program stresses things child can do to make home safe—pick up his skates, don't tie string across a doorway, and so on. Age: preschool to teen-age. Various times; live/film/tape; 2 cameras; 1 hour rehearsal; 2½ hours preparation.

JOHNNY BE CAREFUL. How children can live and play safely in their neighborhoods, on school grounds, and at home, is main burden of this program. Cartoon and safety skit (live or film) are regular features. Children appear when program content requires. Script is prepared by Director of Safety Division of Jackson City Police Department. Age: preschool to 9. Saturday mornings; 15 minutes; live/film/tape; 1 camera; ½ to 1½ hours rehearsal; 8 hours writing and preparation. Sponsored.

SWIMMING POOL SAFETY. Annual program of swimming instruction and water safety is broadcast from full-size pool on station property. Red Cross and YMCA swimming instructors show youngsters how to conduct themselves in and around pools, lakes, streams, rivers, and the ocean. Informational films are also shown. Red Cross and YMCA cooperate on production. Age: preschool to teens. Annual (day, time, and length vary); live/film; 2 cameras; 1 hour rehearsal; 2½ hours writing and preparation.

Johnstown, Pennsylvania

HEAVEN SPEAKS. Dramatic religious presentations are interspersed with color slides of inspirational subjects. A Baptist minister produces the program in consultation with Catholic, Jewish, and Protestant clergy. Age: preschool through adult. Sunday afternoon; 15 minutes; live; 2 cameras; 1 hour rehearsal; 5 hours preparation.

Los Angeles, California

FOR WHICH WE STAND. Two hour-long specials that followed a group of 12 sixth graders on their week's tour of Washington, D.C. The students, two from each of the city's six school districts, were chosen because of their understanding of democracy and student government experience. Accompanying them were a teacher-guide, a tutor (required by law to tutor the children 3 hours a day during the trip), a registered nurse, and a station camera crew. Students attended four preparatory sessions before departure. Project sponsored by station. Age: 6 to 12. Prime evening time; Tuesday and Wednesday; 1 hour; film. Sponsored.

Milwaukee, Wisconsin

GUIDEPOSTS FOR YOUTH. Informal religious and educational program conducted by a local Lutheran school principal. Children take part in panel discussions, conduct scientific experiments, and exhibit their arts and crafts. Missionaries, educators, and ministers are guests and Lutheran mission films are shown occasionally. Age: 6 to 12. Sunday morning; 30 minutes; tape; 2 cameras; 5 hours rehearsal; 10 hours preparation.

Minneapolis, Minnesota

BIBLE STORY TIME. Children act out short vignettes on topics such as selfishness. Then the clergyman-host tells a story related to the vignette and questions the children on its meaning. Hand puppets and rear projections are used occasionally. The Central Lutheran School and Bible Education, Inc., of St. Paul supply talent and props. Program is video taped for distribution in the United States and Canada by Bible Education, Inc. Age: preschool to 12. Sunday morning; half-hour; live; 2 cameras; 11 hours rehearsal; 21 hours writing and preparation.

New Britain, Connecticut

CHILDREN'S HOUR. Puppets, films, toys, story books, and records are used by host as he takes young audience on visits around the world. Produced by Council of Churches, program aims to teach brotherhood, respect for others, and reverence. Alternate Sundays; 30 minutes.

New Haven, Connecticut

ROY CARLEY SHOW. On this Bible quiz program, the host draws a cartoon representing a phrase from the Bible, and the children guess what the phrase is and where it appears. Setting is a den with drawing board. Protestant members of the station's advisory board devised the program at station request, and state and city church councils cooperate on production. Age: 6 to 12. Saturday morning; 15 minutes; tape; 2 cameras; 6 hours rehearsal; 6½ hours preparation.

VISITING SISTERS OF THE IMMACULATE CONCEPTION. A nun prepares short Bible story skits involving 12 children and then questions them on the history of Catholicism. Catholic members of the station's advisory board devised the program at the request of the station, and the Roman Catholic Archdiocese of Hartford cooperates on production. Age: preschool to 9. Saturday morning; 15 minutes; live/tape; 6½ hours rehearsal; 6½ hours preparation.

New York, New York

LET'S TALK ABOUT GOD. Two Maryknoll sisters use puppets to dramatize Christian principles and Catholic teachings. A sample vignette examined the meaning of names (such as Hilary, which means "cheerful") and the effect one's name might have on his personality and way of life. Program is produced under auspices of the Roman Catholic Archdiocese of New York. Age: preschool to 9. Sunday morning; 15 minutes; live; 3 cameras; 3 hours rehearsal; 13 hours preparation.

JEWISH FOURTH R. Program is keyed to the Jewish calendar. On Jewish holidays representative songs and dances are presented, and the narrator describes the historical and religious background of the festival. Nonholiday programs adhere to religious school routine with children answering a rabbi's questions. The New York Board of Rabbis cooperates on production. Age: 6 to 12. Sunday morning; 15 minutes; live/tape; 3 cameras; 3 hours rehearsal; 13 hours preparation.

PROTESTANT FOURTH R. In this Bible-story game, the host tells a story and then puts questions to two teams of children of elementary school age. As correct answers are given a game board reveals letters of a key word. The first team to guess the key word wins. The Protestant Council of the City of New York coordinates the selection of participants and subject matter. Age: 6 to 12. Sunday morning; 15 minutes; live; 3 cameras; 13 hours preparation.

Oklahoma City, Oklahoma

SUNDAY SCHOOL. The teacher uses pictures, short stories with a moral, stories of the life of Christ, and a dancing doll to impart each week's message. Though children do not participate, the teacher shows pictures and reads letters submitted by viewers. The Oklahoma City Council of Churches advises on production. Age: 6 to 9. Sunday morning; half-hour; live; 2 cameras; half-hour rehearsal; 2 hours preparation.

Philadelphia, Pennsylvania

THE GENE LONDON SHOW. Around-the-week program of news, exercises, arts and crafts instruction, stories, guest performers, and guests with animals. Films and cartoons are included. The Board of Education, Zoological Garden, a dance academy, and The Franklin Institute provide guests and materials. Age: preschool to 9. Monday through Friday, 55 minutes; Saturday and Sunday, 1 hour; tape/film; 2 cameras; 3 hours rehearsal; 8 hours preparation.

Pittsburgh, Pennsylvania

SUNDAY CHURCH SCHOOL. Actual Sunday school class filmed "on location." Every effort is made to retain authenticity. This series produced in cooperation with the Pittsburgh Council of Churches, which selects the church to be featured during the month. Age: 6 to 12. Sundays; ½ hour; film; 3½ hours preparation.

Portland, Maine

TV BIBLE SCHOOL. A two-week, daily program to acquaint children and their parents with the Bible. Presented by Parent-Educator Section of Confraternity of Christian Doctrine, program consists of stories from the Bible told by a storyteller. Children participate, acting out portions of stories, singing hymns, or just listening. Age: preschool to 12; parents. Monday through Friday; ½ hour; live; 2 cameras; 30 minutes rehearsal; 1 hour preparation.

Providence, Rhode Island

TV CHURCH SCHOOL. Hostess and five children sing hymns, work on projects, ask and answer questions on religious subjects, read Bible stories, and do costumed pantomimes of an event from the Bible. Children's choirs and representatives of member units are frequent guests. The Rhode Island State Council of Churches cooperates on production. Age: 6 to 9. Sunday morning; half-hour; live/tape; 2 cameras; 2½ hours rehearsal; 7 hours preparation.

Roanoke, Virginia

WONDERFUL WORLD. Hour-long program of news and current events edited for children and supported by maps and charts, spiritual discussions by a young minister and the studio audience, physical fitness demonstrations, spelling bees, community sings, arts and crafts, puppet shows, and Encyclopaedia Britannica films. Age: 6 to 12. Saturday morning; 1 hour; live/film; 2 cameras; half-hour rehearsal; 10 hours writing and preparation. Sponsored.

Omaha, Nebraska

DEAR SANTA. Single Christmas program. A narrator read the famous "Yes, Virginia, there is a Santa Claus" editorial and children's letters to Santa, and Catholic, Protestant, and Jewish clergymen discussed the meaning of Christmas and Hanukkah. Carol singing and a film of Mahalia Jackson singing gospels were included. The First Methodist Church, Holy Name Parish, and Temple Israel of Omaha cooperated on production. Age: preschool to high school. One time only; half-hour; live/film; 3 cameras; 3 hours rehearsal; 10 hours writing and preparation.

JEAN'S STORY TIME. The teacher tells a Bible story using slides and film strips which are shown through a story window (replica of a stained glass window).

Then the children read Bible verses appropriate to the story. Since the program tries to attract children who are shut-ins or "unchurched," the teacher reads the names of new viewers and adds their pictures to the set's storyboard. Lutheran ministers and laymen help with production, and the head of the University of Omaha's television department is program editor. Age: preschool to 12. Sunday morning; half-hour; live; 2 cameras; 3 hours rehearsal; 29 hours preparation.

San Diego, California

HOUSE OF HAPPINESS. A children's religious program that utilizes the animated "Davey and Goliath" film series in lieu of straight entertainment film. In the live segments, groups of children participate in songs, puppet shows, drawing, and other group activities. Films are supplied through the National Council of Churches in cooperation with station. Age: preschool to 12. Saturday mornings; 30 minutes; tape/film.

San Francisco, California

ADVENTURE SCHOOL. This program of entertainment and information for preschoolers and their mothers is reported to have pioneered the nursery school format. Viewer participation activities and work with children in the studio demonstrate the teaching techniques developed by the teacher, Marian Koehler Rowe (founder and director of Adventure School in North Hollywood and nationally known for her work in parent education). She gives advice to mothers and compares experiences in child raising with parents, teachers, child psychologists, and counselors who visit the program. The Association for Nursery Education and the Family Life Education Committee of San Francisco are among cooperating groups. Age: preschool. Monday through Friday morning; half-hour; live/tape; 2 cameras; half-hour rehearsal; 4 hours writing and preparation. Sponsored.

CHILDREN AND GOD. A children's religious series that demonstrates the services of worship and typical Sunday school class activities of as many as twenty-six faiths. Children and teachers of various churches and temples participated. Age: 10 to 12. Sunday morning; 1 hour; tape; 2 cameras; 6 hours rehearsal; 1 to 2 weeks preparation.

South Bend, Indiana

STORY CORNER. A program of religious stories that is produced in conjunction with the county council of churches. Saturdays, 30 minutes.

Tampa, Florida

KIDS' BIBLE CLUB. Religious instruction by a local ordained minister who is also a ventriloquist. He uses puppets to tell stories and give object lessons. Children in the studio audience are quizzed about the lessons and take part in musical games. The setting is a garden with benches. Local church groups provide participants and musical numbers. Age: preschool to 12. Sunday morning; half-hour; live/tape/film; 2 cameras; 5 hours rehearsal; 10 hours writing and preparation.

Multipurpose

Some programs for children serve a variety of purposes through a variety of program segments: exploring, doing, storytelling, orienting, amusing. When the parts are assembled imaginatively, the result can be a constructive fusion of many elements of aesthetic value that would ordinarily be too difficult or too costly to produce as complete programs, or would unduly tax the interest or attention span of the child. The concomitant risk in the children's variety show is a lack of unity that gives the impression of looking through a kaleidoscope: interesting and gay, but meaningless.

The programs described at length in this section reveal that a colorful personality alone is not enough to supply the required unifying force. Nearly all of them make use of a theme to which a number of the segments can be related, thereby giving the program a basic structure. As a result, these programs should not only occupy time and amuse the young viewer but should also enhance his life.

The world is so full of a number of things,
I'm sure we should all be as happy as kings.
                                    Robert Louis Stevenson

The variety program for children can well contain segments which have been discussed in the previous sections of this book. The multipurpose program allows the program director to emphasize many aspects of the activity of children that will be both educational and entertaining.

Indeed, there is an unbroken continuity between learning and entertainment for children. Escape through entertainment, as adults understand and enjoy it, is not a characteristic response of most normal children. Miss Mary Field in her discussion of suitable films for the juvenile audience has observed that "children come to the pictures in order to take an active part in the proceedings. They are perpetually on the move as they follow the action on the screen." (Mary Field, *Good Company*.) A good variety program can entertain children by an appeal to their continuing search for information. Just as the school curriculum, when properly presented, leads children into an awareness of their community and the part they play in it, so can television be the means of leading children to new adventures in information and recreation.

In the review of children's programs under this multipurpose heading it will be observed that the formats depend upon one or more principles of organization to give unity to the program. If the show is seen daily, it is usually recognized in the schedule by the same universal title and resembles a magazine in its continuity. This method of organizing several program ideas has the advantage of easy identification for the children and assists greatly in building an audience.

Young viewers come to know the three or four personalities who readily become their friends. These regular presenters are responsible for the introduction of recurring features such as hobbies, crafts, local news about children and their activities in the community.

The multipurpose program is an excellent medium for the presentation of good children's films. Time spent in review of the many sources of syndicated film is well worthwhile. Film is the best means of presenting children of other lands in their own environment. Travel to these lands by means of film has a wide appeal for children. In addition, storytelling that takes place in a natural setting is best presented on film. One might say that film is most suited for landscape backgrounds, while the television studio is best suited for the more intimate interaction of characters or for close-ups of details, e.g., a science or hobby show. A serialized film is excellent as a regular feature on a daily show. It is less expensive than live dramatic presentation and often more effective, especially since so many stations have limited facilities for elaborate production.

In the selection of film, care should be taken to procure film prints that will have adequate quality when projected on the telecine chain. A "washed-out" or "black" film on the television screen is certain to lose the audience since the picture information is so blurred.

The most important feature of the multipurpose program is the technique employed for continuity. The program must be more than a "basket" or catchall. The director must exercise care to see that there is some visual logic to the sequence of the segments and that one experience moves with meaning and interest to the next. It is hard on the presenters to have to carry the continuity at the verbal level alone. Instead, the presenter and the viewer can share the excitement of unfolding the next events to come in the program, as a close-up of an interesting mobile leads into the craft segment, or a close-up of living creatures in action leads into the natural science segment. More general devices for continuity can be employed, e.g., THE CLOCK SHOW, ANN'S ATTIC, the BREAKFAST CLUB, THE MAGIC TOY SHOP, or the railroad stations in MR. THATCH AND I and DIMPLE DEPOT.

The ultimate success of the multipurpose program depends upon the skill with which the visual sequence is maintained. If the show depends entirely upon an abstract idea, the show itself quickly becomes a cliché. The dangerous abstractions of the "title show" are overcome by careful planning of what should be seen and the order in which it should be seen. The decor should be simple so as not to distract from the subject matter being presented. The verbal commentary should be relevant and it should be kept to a minimum so that the pictures can tell their own story. Most good television is conceived at the planning stage. Splendid studio facilities will not make a good show if the director has not worked out his visual presentation before he comes to the studio.

If the show depends upon personalities too much, the characters lose out because they are too much in the "telling" or the "demonstrative" role. The hosts in the children's show must be emotionally mature men and women who understand the way children respond to adult behavior. The strain of the host who must carry the whole show himself is often revealed in an attitude of condescension. Another desperate mannerism of the adult who is embarrassed by having the whole burden of continuity on his shoulders, and who is often still more confused by his inadequacy in dealing naturally with children, is seen in the showman who seeks to arouse the interest of children by overstimulation with loud voice and ridiculous gestures.

In the end the presenter must know how to invite a normal response from children. He must allow time for these responses. He must share in the planning of the content and be involved in the production of the program so that his young viewers can share in a common experience with him. The child then has a natural confidence in his presenter. Secure in the worth of the information he sees, he develops a real enthusiasm for a world which "is so full of a number of things." These varied experiences are worthy of repetition because the child enjoys a certain satisfaction in a warm familiarity with people and things. Perhaps the real security which a young viewer experiences in a good book, a good television program, or a good game is what Robert Louis Stevenson had in mind when he cherished for all children a kind of joy which should make them all "as happy as kings."

The Totem Club
Chicago, Illinois

Many program series appeal to a wide spectrum of children's interests in every broadcast. THE TOTEM CLUB chooses instead to concentrate on a single subject in the course of each program, thereby providing for a broad variety of interests over a week's time. It is presented for a half-hour in the late afternoon, Monday through Friday, and is directed to children aged 6 to 11.

On Mondays, a real Indian tells Indian stories, teaches dances, and provides guidance for nature study in a set consisting of a tepee and woodland complete with waterfall. Tuesdays are devoted to crafts and cooking: a large book background (and a fanciful talking giraffe) for crafts and a kitchen set for cooking. The Tuesday program is specially designed to include deaf children in the audience.

Wednesday is music day from September to June, with demonstrations of instruments and musical illustrations performed by different sections of the orchestra against an abstract musical background. In the summer, Wednesday is turned over to swimming instruction and baseball tips, for which the studio moves outdoors.

Every Thursday a professional theatre group performs a play especially written for television viewing by children. The Thursday set varies with the play. Friday programs consist of video-taped highlights from previous broadcasts.

The assistance of many organizations is enlisted: the Red Cross for the swimming series; a consumer cooperative for the cooking demonstration; a hobby magazine contributes the handcraft demonstrator; the Chicago Fire Department empties and fills the swimming pool every week during the summer. Upwards of 200 man-hours by station personnel and others go into the production of THE TOTEM CLUB every week.

Ann's Attic
Rochester, New York

Instruction in better ways for youngsters to make use of materials at home and an awareness of community educational, cultural, and industrial resources of interest to children are emphasized in this twice weekly, late afternoon, half-hour "magazine" program for children aged 4 to 9.

An old attic filled with steamer trunks, a player piano, a grandfather clock, an umbrella stand, and some old dress forms provides the setting in which Ann acts as hostess to a group of interesting characters. These include a scarecrow, a tiger, two inquisitive children from "next door," and Mr. Jim, handyman and art instructor. The scope of the program is as broad as the child's interests and local resources—both public and private—permit. Programs are based on materials and projects developed in cooperation with such institutions as the Museum of Arts and Sciences, Public Library, Seneca Park Zoo, Memorial Art Gallery, Eastman School of Music of the University of Rochester, and civic and service organizations.

The attic makes possible finding, explaining, and using artifacts of the present and past, science materials, musical instruments, and books. Visitors who come to call can discuss news events and community happenings of interest to children.

A key role is taken by Mr. Jim, art consultant for the area school district, who draws murals on the wall to music, illustrates stories as they are told, and instructs the children in the use of art materials familiar to them.

A measure of audience response to ANN's ATTIC came following a program that included a sequence with live birds from the zoo. The children were asked to draw pictures of the birds and send them to the station. No prizes or premiums were offered. More than 5,000 pieces of mail were received.

Marshal J
San Francisco, California

The natural interest of children in cowboys extends to the real aspects of ranch life—horses, dogs, branding irons, lassoes, the roundup—as well as to the more familiar romanticized heroes of Western fiction. The lore of the West, instruction in rope handling, safety in gun handling are featured daily by the 6-foot, 5-inch host of MARSHAL J, a man who has been on cattle drives, followed the rodeo circuit, owned his own ranches, and was born and raised in the Texas border country, where the memory of frontier days was still fresh. By offering his stories and instruction in a context of first-run cartoons, the Marshal is able to attract a sizable audience and help keep alive an authentic picture of the period and region that made this country's primary contribution to folk history.

The set is a realistic replica of the tack room and stall area of a working ranch. On his first appearance in San Francisco (for seven years he had been host of a similar program in Cedar Rapids, Iowa) he brought along his three-month-old Dalmatian puppy. The children have enjoyed watching the puppy grow and develop since that time.

MARSHAL J is broadcast as an early-evening, half-hour program Monday through Saturday and in a one-hour format Saturday mornings. The county medical association, Morrison Planetarium, Help the Handicapped campaign, and the National Council of Churches are among the organizations assisting in preparing informational material for the program.

The Clock Show

Chicago, Illinois

THE CLOCK SHOW, presented five days a week from 7:30 to 8:30 in the morning, is designed to make it easier for 8- to 12-year-olds to get off to their school chores. Each broadcast contains seven or eight compact segments to give the children something to think about, to wonder at, or to giggle over.

The program is paced for a mobile audience getting dressed; breakfasting; or collecting school books, homework, sweaters, and lunchboxes. In addition to the permanent host and an occasional guest, two youngsters (called "clock watchers") appear. They are chosen from the local schools each week by their principal as a reward for scholastic achievement.

Titles of some of the segments indicate the nature and scope of the material: "Let's Experiment," simple scientific experiments; "Think It Over," thought-provoking problems, solutions to which are given the next day; "Good Looking," art appreciation and fundamentals of drawing; "It Figures," mathematical puzzles; "Minute Mysteries," snap identification of famous people. "Pet Pointers" and "Sure You Can Cook" are typical of other program elements. News and weather reports are regular daily features.

About 50 per cent of each program consists of live informational material, 15 per cent is informational film, 25 per cent is entertainment, with the balance devoted to public service announcements. The program requires some 12 man-hours of preparation each day by the producer, an artist, the host, and a news reporter.

The set contains a desk, maps, and tables. Such institutions as the Chicago Historical Society, Natural History Museum, and Art Institute systematically provide facts and illustrative material.

Mr. Thatch and I
Tulsa, Oklahoma

An old-fashioned train depot, an unclaimed scarecrow, two red squirrels, a book, a film, and a kindly old stationmaster are the components of this weekly Saturday-morning half-hour program.

The pace, befitting a rural whistle stop, is leisurely. The stationmaster (Mr. Clickety Clack) engages in small talk with the scarecrow (Mr. Thatch) who maintains his end of the conversation through a pre-recorded audio tape. At about five minutes into the program the 8:05 fun freight arrives with its weekly cargo: a sack of sunflower seeds for the squirrels, a children's picture story book, a "Davey and Goliath" cartoon from the National Council of Churches, and a guest animal—the pet of the week.

Mr. Clickety Clack feeds the sunflower seeds to the squirrels. (The children like to watch the squirrels in close-up, carefully cracking the shells and fastidiously disposing of them before eating the seeds.) Then he reads from the story book, voice over the pictures on camera. After some further chatting with Mr. Thatch, the film is seen. Finally, the guest arrival is examined, and the next train comes tootling in to signal the end of the broadcast.

The interest of young children in a ritualized performance is pleasantly and wholesomely served in this program.

Fred n Fae Breakfast Club
Denver, Colorado

In a Monday-through-Friday early-morning half-hour series, the FRED N FAE BREAKFAST CLUB combines elements of exploration, doing, orientation, and entertainment. A young man-and-wife team, Fred and Fae, do a "children's newscast" with interpretation, provide weather reports, give news of children's clubs, interview club officers, encourage good personal habits, and conduct essay contests.

A contest in January, 1962, was introduced in these words: "Let's each think of some way to help make our world a better place. You have heard us explain about the world problems on our newscast each morning. We know there are problems in Berlin, problems about Communism, bomb testing, fallout shelters, and closer to home, problems about integration. We would like to have each of you pick out one of these problems and write down what you think should be done about it. You can discuss it with your folks or your teacher, but put your solution in your own words." Daily and monthly winners were chosen, prizes awarded, and each day one of the winning essays was read during the newscast.

FRED N FAE BREAKFAST CLUB has been a regular presentation since 1958. Program promotion includes a monthly four-page syndicated magazine containing "things to do" for children and a calendar with habit-and-behavior checklist.

The Magic Toy Shop
Syracuse, New York

The implicit goals of a kindergarten are to stimulate creative play, to introduce the very young to the wonders of the world, to make them aware of strange lands and different peoples, to encourage learning of songs and languages, to help them to cope with new experiences. This half-hour program broadcast five times a week employs the resources of television to reach for many of the kindergarten's goals and, in some respects, to go beyond.

The setting of this multipurpose program is a toy shop complete with trains and giant blocks (the largest is six feet tall), a piano and a movie projector, toys and clowns, plus a make-believe area that changes every day. The cast consists of Merrily, the toy shop proprietress; Eddie Flum Num, her chief assistant, who shows movies and sketches for stories; Twinkle, a clown who plays the piano and talks wordlessly only in music; Floogie, the general of the toys; Mr. Trolly, who tells stories; and the Play Lady, who visits on occasion to introduce the children to new toys.

The program goes outside the studio to film news from the United Nations, to the barber or the dentist, a visit to a pottery factory, and to video-tape a dancer from Nigeria, baby animals, or a German zither player.

The program, broadcast since February, 1955, has developed out of extensive planning with representatives appointed by the PTA, Mothers' Club Federation, Syracuse University's Department of Preschool Education, and the Children's Division of the Public Library. (Continuing interest in the program is also demonstrated by sponsors, one of which, a local shoe store, has been an advertiser ever since the first broadcast.)

Dimple Depot
Pittsburgh, Pennsylvania

The stationmaster of DIMPLE DEPOT has a wide circle of friends who call on him regularly: a policeman and a fireman, who present safety skits; a guitar-playing folk singer, who sings and tells stories; a magician. Two other regular residents are a bat puppet, who lives in an old-fashioned wall telephone, and a dog. In addition to managing the comings and goings at the depot, Mr. Dimple illustrates the stories told by his guests. He uses a large sketch pad attached by a pantograph to the wall near his desk.

The set is a realistic reconstruction of a turn-of-the-century way station. A bay-window area is useful for incorporating action taking place outside the station; an open floor area in the center of the station and a bench along one wall provide sitting and performing space for the guests.

DIMPLE DEPOT, which is broadcast Monday through Friday afternoons, is a completely live program. Film clips are occasionally used to illustrate an activity that could not easily be reproduced in the studio (safety practices in crossing the street, for example), but film segments are not a regular part of the program. The Pittsburgh Junior League cooperates in the production of the program, and three times a week the Carnegie Library helps produce a 15- to 20-minute segment consisting of art, music, ballet, marionettes, or stories.

Most of the material is at the preschool through first grade level, but the producers try to "include anything which we feel will stimulate the child's mind, even if he doesn't absorb it all."

105

The Skipper Ryle Show
Cincinnati, Ohio

The river motif is strong in Cincinnati's history, as it is in many cities and towns along the Ohio. Like other historic routes, it suggests access to the outside world: a two-way avenue by which to leave in order to see the world and by which to bring elements of the world back.

"Skipper" Ryle, the amiable pilot of the mythical *River Queen,* employs this motif in a two-hour Sunday morning program, which includes stories about the River, the Old West, and the Civil War; news edited for children; Bible stories; a science quiz; suggestions for the care of pet animals; musical, dramatic, and dance acts by young performers; and a variety of special features, with heavy emphasis on travel and learning about life in other parts of the world.

Skipper Ryle's "specials" have included a trip to Hawaii, with native Hawaiian music, dances and stories; a tour of Paris, with sightseeing; a visit to "your island" in the Caribbean, with calypso, the Limbo, and a steel band; and "Christmas around the World," with music, song, and dance by children from many countries. In a homelier vein, one entire hour was devoted to fire prevention (produced on location), and a two-hour Air Force "special" was filmed at Wright-Patterson Air Force Base in Dayton.

Program formats and sets vary, depending upon the featured subject matter. The Cincinnati Steamship Society, the Zoological Society, the Simian Society, the Veterinary Association, United States Army, Navy, Marines, and Air Force, and the Cincinnati Council of Churches are among the regularly cooperating groups.

Albany, Georgia

CAPTAIN MERCURY AND THE SPACE EXPLORERS. An audience of 25 children, passengers in a rocket ship temporarily at rest in a spaceport on the planet Zeus, share the camera with five cartoons daily. Children are interviewed, operate the space control board, put on skits, promote local and space club activities. Special film feature includes "Tomorrow the World," of USAF space series. Age: preschool to 9. Monday through Friday; 50 minutes; live/film; 2 cameras; 15 minutes rehearsal; 1 hour preparation. Sponsored.

Albuquerque, New Mexico

K CIRCLE B TIME. Program of Roy Rogers and Gene Autry films is also vehicle for promoting 4-H, United Fund, scouting, and other community activities. Occasional guests—for example, a glass blower. About 35 children in studio audience; sometimes participate in song or skit. Birthdays recognized, contests promoted ("win a pony"). Age: 6 to 12. Monday through Friday; 1 hour and 25 minutes; live/tape/film; 2 cameras; 1 hour preparation. Sponsored.

Altoona, Pennsylvania

BREAKFAST TIME. General conversation between host and puppets plus cartoons and guests. Puppets do record pantomimes and work through picture window of breakfast-bar setting. Age: 5 to 15. Monday through Friday morning; 45 minutes; live/film; 1 camera; 1 hour writing and preparation. Sponsored.

HOURIGAN'S HOOLIGANS. Children's club meeting on the air complete with minutes of last meeting, old business, new business (scout meetings, church affairs). Drawing contests conducted and entries displayed. Comedy films. Age: 6 to 12. Mondays, Wednesdays, Fridays; 30 minutes; live/film; 2 cameras; 1 hour preparation. Sponsored.

SY SEAWEED'S POPEYE PLAYHOUSE. Young studio guests chat with captain host, play word and hand games, sing songs, and watch Popeye cartoons. Setting is a dockside boathouse. Age: preschool to 9. Monday through Friday; 25 minutes; 2 cameras; live/film; 1 hour preparation. Sponsored.

Atlanta, Georgia

THE BILLY JOHNSON SHOW. Host sings and plays the guitar, works with puppets, shows pictures submitted by children, and urges protection of wildlife and forests. Cartoons are shown. "Lazy River" setting with a log cabin and lakeside scene. State and national forestry organizations help on production

107

and supply "Smokey Bear" kits to viewers on request. Age: preschool to 12. Monday through Friday, 2 hours (in two separate sections); Saturday, 30 minutes; live/film; 2 cameras; 30 minutes rehearsal; 4 hours writing and preparation. Sponsored.

Austin, Texas

UNCLE JAY SHOW. Live portion of this late afternoon program includes interviews with guest children, performances by local talent, physical fitness demonstrations, puppetry, and pictures drawn to music. Informational and entertainment films fill out the hour and a quarter. Age: 4 to 14. Monday through Friday; 1¼ hours; 2 cameras; live/tape/film; 10 minutes rehearsal; 6½ hours preparation. Sponsored.

Baton Rouge, Louisiana

BUCKSKIN BILL. In this program of frontier days, an Indian scout host tells true stories of the American pioneer and talks with members of the Cub Scouts, Boy Scouts, and Recreation and Park Commission. Cartoons are also shown. Setting is a frontier cabin with potbellied stove, water barrel, and animal traps. Age: 10 and up. Monday through Friday afternoon; 1 hour; live/tape/film; 2 cameras; 3 hours preparation. Sponsored.

STORYLAND. Indian scout host entertains young viewers with stories, games, and animals in a country store setting. Popeye, Bugs Bunny, and other cartoons are shown. Age: preschool. Monday through Friday; 30 minutes; live/tape/film; 2 cameras; 2 hours writing and preparation. Sponsored.

Beaumont, Texas

UNCLE WILLIE'S CARTOON CLUB. The host presides over a morning program of Popeye, Warner Bros., and Merrie Melodies cartoons with the help of a child who is host or hostess for the day. Members of youth organizations often make a brief appearance on the program. Age: preschool to 12. Monday through Friday; 30 minutes; 2 cameras; tape/film; 30 minutes rehearsal; 4 to 5 hours preparation. Sponsored.

Binghamton, New York

ADMIRAL'S BIRTHDAY PARTY. Admiral Appleby, host of POPEYE AND THE ADMIRAL, and puppet assistant entertain 50 to 100 children having birthdays in the current month with games and prizes. Celebrities and groups like the Korean Orphans' Choir make special appearances. Age 4 to 12. Friday; 30 minutes; live/film; 2 cameras; 30 minutes rehearsal; 5 hours writing and preparation. Sponsored.

POPEYE AND THE ADMIRAL. Admiral host and a chicken puppet entertain viewers, exhibit art work submitted by children, and show cartoons. Regular features promote local cultural resources for children. Setting is a barge tied up to a wharf. Age: preschool to 12. Monday, Wednesday, and Friday; 30 minutes; live/film; 2 cameras; 1 hour rehearsal; 3 hours preparation. Sponsored.

Birmingham, Alabama

BUGS BUNNY SHOW WITH BENNY CARLE. Studio audience participates in games, jokes, songs, and interviews. Birthday children are put in spotlight. Bugs Bunny and other cartoons are shown, and setting is a forest with life-size cartoon figures. Age: preschool to 12. Monday through Friday afternoon; 30 minutes; live/film; 2 cameras; 30 minutes rehearsal; 30 minutes writing and preparation. Sponsored.

Boise, Idaho

LITTLE JOE THE BRAKEMAN. Brakeman costume of host, caboose set, and freight train sound effects introduce list of popular cartoons: Felix, Bozo, Deputy Dawg, Clutch Cargo, Casper, Heckle and Jeckle, Super Cat. Host also keeps a birthday book, discusses safety and public service programs, conducts drawing contests, and displays children's entries. Age: 6 to 12. Monday through Friday; 1 hour; live; 2 cameras; 1 hour rehearsal; 6 hours preparation. Sponsored.

Boston, Massachusetts

BIG BROTHER WITH BOB EMERY. Drawing contests, salutes to a current holiday, and guest interviews alternate with cartoons and films showing the culture and resources of various countries. Children's Cancer Research Foundation and youth organizations are associated with the program. Age: preschool to 12. Monday through Saturday; 30 minutes; live/tape/film; 2 cameras; 30 minutes rehearsal; 3 hours preparation. Sponsored.

BOOMTOWN WITH REX TRAILER. This lengthy weekend program introduces New England children to life in the West. Host and Mexican friend tell true stories of the West, show the audience how to tie ropes and handle animals, and lead youngsters in games and cowboy skits. Program moves outdoors in warm weather to street setting of a Western town with general store, corral, sheriff's office, and opera house, and includes outdoor demonstrations of fire-fighting and fire-rescue techniques. During cold months the setting is a western bunkhouse interior. Program format includes cartoons and films including station-produced features that explore life in foreign countries. An official of the Massachusetts Society for the Prevention of Cruelty to Animals conducts a regular "Critter Corner" segment with live animals. Age: 6 to 12. Saturday, 3 hours; Sunday, 2½ hours; live/film/tape; 2 cameras; 2 hours rehearsal; 20 hours preparation. Sponsored.

THE CAPTAIN BOB SHOW. Nature stories, drawing lessons, scrambled-word and guess-what contests, puppets, skits, and songs, make up the live portion —or two-thirds—of this program. Balance is cartoon fare, mainly "Clutch Cargo." Fishing-shack set is crammed with appropriate props—nets, lobster traps, oars, etc. Local groups participate in program to promote their services. Age: preschool to 12. Saturdays; 1½ hours; live/tape/film; 2 cameras; 4 hours rehearsal; 15 hours writing and preparation. Sponsored.

S.S. POPEYE. Aboard an old sailing ship, sea captain host with children as crew entertains audience with sea stories and simple instructions in how to comb their hair, polish their shoes, brush their teeth, and so on. Popeye cartoons are integrated with games and stories. Age: preschool to 9; Saturdays; 1 hour; live/film; 2 cameras; 1 hour rehearsal; 5 hours writing and preparation. Sponsored.

Bristol, Virginia

LOONEY TUNES CLUB. Program of interviews, patter, and entertainment film presented before studio audience of 35 children. Children interviewed occasionally have joke to tell or picture to show of their family or pets. Carnival atmosphere. Age: 6 to 12. Monday through Friday; 25 minutes; live/film; 2 cameras; 1 hour rehearsal; 2 hours preparation. Sponsored.

THE POPEYE SHOW. Sailor host reads mail received from viewers, gives announcements about school activities, and shows cartoons. Guests of interest to young children appear occasionally. Age: preschool. Monday through Friday; 25 minutes; live/film; 2 cameras; 2 hours rehearsal; 1 hour preparation. Sponsored.

Buffalo, New York

CAPTAIN BOB. From a ship-deck and tropical-island setting, the host comments on current topics, presents young performers, chats with prominent personalities, and discusses the habits and care of animals with a veterinarian and science-museum director. Cartoons are included. Age: preschool to early teens. Monday through Friday afternoon; 1 hour; live/film; 2 cameras; 30 minutes rehearsal; 5½ hours writing and preparation. Sponsored.

Cedar Rapids, Iowa

THE DR. MAX SHOW. Stories, games, pets, and souvenirs related to the host's travels alternate with tips on safety, proper behavior, and animal care. Cartoons and films are included. Age: preschool to 12. Monday and Friday, 1½ hours; Tuesday through Thursday, 1 hour; live/film; 2 cameras; 45 minutes rehearsal; 5 hours preparation. Sponsored.

Champaign, Illinois

CARTOON TIME. Weekly program featuring magic tricks, a company of puppets (Calvin Caterpillar, Commodore Spintop, Sarge the Dog), and a host with training in drama and music. Cartoons include samplings from international film festivals. Age: preschool to 9. Sundays; 30 minutes; tape/film; 2 cameras; 2 hours rehearsal; 17 hours writing and preparation.

Charleston, South Carolina

HAPPY RAINE SHOW. Local entertainment interspersed with cartoons. Hostess introduces child guests, announces birthdays, conducts contests on the air, reports events of interest to youngsters. Children occasionally perform. Indian setting with forest scene, trees, totem pole, grass. Age: preschool to 12. Monday through Saturday—Monday and Friday, ¾ hour; Tuesday, Wednesday, Thursday, ¼ hour; Saturday, ½ hour; live/film; 2 cameras; ½ hour rehearsal. Sponsored.

Charlotte, North Carolina

CLOWN CARNIVAL. Children ride a working carousel and cavort with the clown-host in a carnival setting. Program includes drawing contests, performances by members of local chapter of National Clown's Club, visits with officials of Charlotte Mint Museum, films, and cartoons. Age: 3 to 12. Monday through Friday; 1 hour; live/film; 2 cameras; 30 minutes rehearsal; 3 hours preparation. Sponsored.

Chicago, Illinois

HERE'S GERALDINE. A giraffe puppet presides over a puppet menagerie in a program of dramatizations, music, stories, poetry, pet care tips, and cartoons. Puppeteers are a husband-and-wife team. No studio audience, but children's art work and poetry sent in to the program and displayed and read on the air. The local Anti-cruelty Society provides guests with interesting pets. Age: preschool. Monday through Friday; 30 minutes; live/tape/film; 2 cameras; 1½ hours rehearsal; 4 hours writing and preparation. Sponsored.

THE JOBBLEWOCKY PLACE. A variety program built around a ventriloquist, who has 14 different "dummies" that he uses in turn to dramatize simple story situation ("going to a party," "a day in school," etc.). Host also performs drawing tricks with letters of alphabet, showing how they can be transformed into pictures of objects or cartoons. Simple craft demonstrated occasionally; one cartoon (Felix or Betty Boop) each program. Set includes topsy-turvy living room, "wreck" room, etc., with upside-down tables. Age: preschool to 12. Monday through Friday; ½ hour; live/film; 2 cameras; 1½ hours rehearsal; 5 to 6 hours writing and preparation. Sponsored.

Chico, California

DON'S CARTOON CLUB. Nutty Squirrels, Bozo the Clown, Harvey Cartoons, Clutch Cargo, and Topsy Turvy Theatre cartoons alternate with live portions, which include drawing instructions and children's demonstrations of puppetry, magic, and drawing. Local PTA's and scout groups participate in programming. Age: preschool to 9. Monday through Friday; 45 minutes; live/film; 2 cameras; 1 hour rehearsal; 1½ hours preparation. Sponsored.

Cincinnati, Ohio

COMMANDER 12. From the master control center of his orbiting space ship, Commander 12 keeps young viewers up to date on events in outer space. He discusses the stars and planets, has adventures with space puppets, and shows Encyclopaedia Britannica and Air Force Film Library films. The USAF also provides program material and copy. Age: preschool to 9. Monday through Friday; 1 hour; live/film; 1 camera; 3 hours preparation. Sponsored.

MR. HOP. Six-foot white-rabbit host and a friend (either Artie the Mouse, Otto the Toy Soldier, or Alex the Court Jester) develop simple program theme—a search for a magic box or a trip back in time to dinosaur age. Visual effects and story from Story Corner tied to theme. Mr. Hop's friend usually does a dance or two; one or two cartoons are also featured. Age: preschool. Saturdays; 1 hour; tape/film; 2 cameras; 1 hour rehearsal; 18 hours writing and preparation. Sponsored.

Cleveland, Ohio

BARNABY, POPEYE, AND FRIENDS. Daily program of stories and cartoons. Friday programs contain 10 to 15 minutes of news for children supported by films from *Great Headlines of the Century* series and Encyclopaedia Britannica Films. Age: preschool to 9. Monday through Friday afternoon; 35 minutes; live/film; 2 cameras; 45 minutes rehearsal; 12 hours writing and preparation. Sponsored.

CAPTAIN PENNY NOON SHOW. Each program contains video-taped sections on such topics as sports, science, natural history, visits to the zoo, antiques, and linen manufacture, in addition to cartoon format. Occasional guest cartoonist demonstrates drawing tricks. Police and Fire Departments, Health Museum, Animal Protective League, Zoo, Red Cross, and Scouts cooperate. Age: 6 to 12. Monday through Friday; 50 minutes; live/tape/film; 2 cameras; 3 hours writing and preparation. Sponsored.

Colorado Springs, Colorado

BLINKY THE CLOWN. Safety program in a circus setting. Children are interviewed by Blinky, sing the Blinky Safety Song, and report on their safety activities and daily good deed. Guest policemen and safety patrolmen promote safety on streets, sidewalks, and bicycles. Age: preschool to 9. Monday through Friday; 55 minutes; live/film; 2 cameras; 1¼ hours rehearsal; 2 hours preparation. Sponsored.

Columbia, South Carolina

JOLLY JIM SHOW. Good (Jolly Jim) always triumphs over evil (J. P. Sidewinder) in the story line of this program. Popeye, Dick Tracy, travel films, Davey and Goliath cartoons are used liberally. Safety is stressed in program segment produced in cooperation with city Police Department. Many community organizations associated with production. Juvenile audience sits on bleachers in rustic country general-store setting. Age: preschool to 12. Wednesday and Friday afternoons, ½ hour; Saturday mornings, 1 hour; live/tape/film; 2 to 3 cameras; 3 hours rehearsal; 3 to 6 hours writing and preparation. Sponsored.

Columbus, Ohio

CASPER CAPERS. Hosts intersperse cartoon portions with patter, puppetry, skits, and guest interviews. Age: family. Monday through Friday; 1 hour; live/film; 1 camera; 30 minutes rehearsal; 1 hour preparation. Sponsored.

CINDERELLA AND HER FRIENDS. Cinderella's friends are preschoolers who dance, sing, play, watch the hostess draw, and listen to her songs and stories. News reports, educational films, and cartoons complete the format. Age: preschool. Monday through Friday; 1 hour; live/film; 1 camera; 2 hours rehearsal; 8 hours preparation. Sponsored.

DINNER THEATRE. Children demonstrate their hobbies: ham radio rig, photographs, model cars, antique salt-and-pepper-shaker collection. Cartoons are shown. Setting is a den-recreation room. Age: 10 through teens. Monday through Friday evening; 25 minutes; live/film; 1 camera; 2 to 3 hours rehearsal; 1 to 3 hours preparation. Sponsored.

Luci's toyshop. Hostess-proprietor of the toyshop spends a busy half-hour keeping her puppet characters in line, developing program's "situation," demonstrating crafts, reading stories, singing songs. Educational film or cartoon usually shown each program; "live" guests from zoo, Board of Education, service departments of city, appear regularly. Age: preschool. Monday through Friday; ½ hour; live/tape/film; 1 camera; 1 hour rehearsal; 13 hours writing and preparation. Sponsored.

Dallas, Texas

Party time. An audience participation program of games, stunts and songs, interspersed with cartoons and educational features on the zoo, safety, school activities, and good citizenship. Police Department, Citizens Traffic Commission, Zoo, service clubs, public school system, PTA's participate. Age: 6 to 9. Monday through Friday afternoon; 30 minutes; live/tape/film; 2 cameras; half-hour studio rehearsal; 8 hours preparation. Sponsored.

Mr. peppermint. Mr. Peppermint, owner of a music shop and candy counter, describes the daily activities of the inanimate citizens of Goodtown through folk songs, cutouts of song characters, and puppet episodes. Preschool instruction and finger games are held in the Creative Corner. Cartoons and films are included and guests appear occasionally. Age: preschool to 9. Monday through Friday; 1 hour; live/tape/film; 2 cameras; 15 minutes rehearsal; 6 hours preparation. Sponsored.

Dayton, Ohio

Popeye theatre with whittlin' jake and uncle orrie. A daily, 90-minute, late-afternoon presentation of cartoons, songs, comedy skits, clown routines, "how-to" demonstrations, travel films, elementary science experiments, skin diving, and water-safety techniques. Museum of Natural History, Boy Scouts, YMCA, and Model Builders Group are among cooperating organizations. Age: 8 to 16. Monday through Friday; 1½ hours; live/film; 2 cameras; 1½ hours rehearsal; 2 hours writing and preparation. Sponsored.

Denver, Colorado

Fred n fae. Information and entertainment in a birthday party atmosphere. Twelve children attend a studio birthday party complete with refreshments, cartoons, films, and dancing. Coloring and drawing contests are held for viewers and an advice-to-parents segment is included. Police Department,

YWCA, YMCA, Scouts, and American Legion cooperate. Age: preschool to 14. Monday through Friday; 1 hour; live/film; 2 cameras; 15 minutes rehearsal; 12 hours writing and preparation. Sponsored.

Detroit, Michigan

JOHNNY GINGER SHOW. Cartoon program held together by patter and pantomime of host. Occasional young guests include Cub and Brownie Scouts. Age: preschool to 12. Monday through Friday; mornings, 1 hour; afternoons, 30 minutes; live/tape/film; 2 cameras; 1½ hours rehearsal; 4 hours writing and preparation. Sponsored.

KOOKIE KAT. Space ship is setting for live portion of program, which consists of puppet skits involving Kookie Kat (girl) and several comic characters in outer space. One-half of program is taken up with cartoons. Age: preschool to 12. Saturdays; 30 minutes; tape/film; 2 cameras; 1½ hours rehearsal; 7 hours writing and preparation. Sponsored.

MILKY'S PARTY TIME. Milky the Clown, program host, leads his young audience through a round of games (potato and sausage relays), entertains them with magic tricks and Diver Dan cartoons, gives them safety tips, and judges their performing talents. Age: 6 to teens. Saturdays; 1½ hours; live/film; 3 cameras; 9 hours rehearsal; 28 hours writing and preparation. Sponsored.

Q. T. HUSH WITH RICKY THE CLOWN. Clown host sings, draws pictures, and leads studio children in games and contests. Cartoons are interspersed throughout the program. Setting is a "fun" schoolhouse. Scout organizations provide young guests. Age: 6 to 12. Sunday morning; 30 minutes; tape/film; 2 cameras; 11 hours writing and preparation. Sponsored.

Durham, North Carolina

THE CARTOON SHOP. A toy-soldier host, a real dog, and a pretend rabbit (costumed adult) lead a menagerie of puppets in a program of magic acts, dog tricks, songs, patter, stories, drawings, and lessons on good manners and health. Cartoons are also shown. The Junior League, Children's Museum, and Raleigh Little Theater are among the cooperating groups. Age: preschool. Monday through Friday; 1 hour; live/tape/film; 2 cameras; 4 hours preparation. Sponsored.

Eugene, Oregon

JACK'S KARTOON CLUBHOUSE. A crude but actual tree house is setting of this program of Bugs Bunny, Bozo, and other cartoons. Child guests are interviewed and local dancing classes or Brownie troops may present skits, dance, or sing. Program is also vehicle for promoting local events of interest to children and their parents. Age: 6 to 9. Mondays, Wednesdays, Fridays, 1 hour; Tuesdays, Thursdays, ½ hour; live/film; 2 cameras; 45 minutes rehearsal; about 10 hours preparation. Sponsored.

Evansville, Indiana

LUNCH WITH UNCLE DUDLEY. Uncle Dudley is a bespectacled owner of a cartoon shop, and surrounded by his ceramic animal friends he ad-libs a fantasy-seasoned monologue on such topics as planting seeds and inspecting tricycles for safety. Some topics are supported with educational films. Age: preschool to 9. Monday through Friday; 20 minutes; live/film; 2 cameras; 2 hours preparation. Sponsored.

Flint, Michigan

RAE DEANE AND FRIENDS. On this morning variety hour, the hostess, who is an experienced teacher, reads stories, plays the piano and sings, shows how to make valentines, plastic bottle dolls, etc., and chats with two puppets. Guests from Police and Fire Departments talk about safety habits. Live animals are shown occasionally, and simple weather forecasts are given. Cartoons are included. Age: preschool. Monday through Friday; 1 hour; 2 cameras; live/tape/film; 30 minutes rehearsal; 8 hours preparation. Sponsored.

Florence, Alabama

PLANET 15. Cartoons and Davey and Goliath films are shown live audience in "space" set. Host interviews the 10 to 20 spectators, representatives of different schools or Sunday schools. Age: preschool to 12. Monday through Friday; 45 minutes; live/film; 2 cameras. Sponsored.

Fort Dodge, Iowa

UNCLE DICK'S FUN HOUSE. Host draws cartoons, gives drawing instructions, interviews guests, and presides over studio birthday parties. Industrial science shows, visits with Scouts, and handicraft exhibits are periodic special features. Cartoons and films are included. Age: preschool to 12. Monday through Friday; 1 hour; live/film; 1 to 2 cameras. Sponsored.

Fort Wayne, Indiana

THE POPEYE SHOW. Puppet skits, interviews with celebrities, filmed trips to the zoo, and a regular Wednesday visit from a zoologist with the "animal of the week" supplement cartoon series. Elementary schools supervisor, college art instructor, zoologist are consultants on program content. Age: 4 to 12. Monday through Friday early evening; 1 hour; live/tape/film; 3 cameras; 1 hour rehearsal; 8½ hours preparation. Sponsored.

Fort Worth, Texas

CARTOON CAPERS WITH MICKEY AND MICHELLE. Turtle puppet twins report local children's news, teach songs, pantomime records, read birthday mail, and interview guests. Settings range from space scene, forest, schoolroom, etc., according to the puppets' adventures. Cartoons are integrated into program content. Age: all. Monday through Friday; 55 minutes; live/film; 2 cameras; 1½ hours rehearsal; 6½ hours preparation. Sponsored.

Fresno, California

FELIX THE CAT. Cartoon program supplemented with host's jokes and patter. The host encourages viewers to send in safety posters, which he displays on the air. Friday evening; 30 minutes; live/film; 2 cameras. Sponsored.

FLIPPO JR. AND POPEYE SHOW. Clown-host shows Popeye cartoons, interviews children, discusses events of interest to youngsters, works with puppets, shows children how to make things, and displays safety posters submitted by viewers. Educational films are also shown. Setting is a home interior with door, telephone, and talking rocking chair. Zoo officials appear as guest experts and discuss animals shown on program. Age: preschool through teens. Monday through Friday; 45 minutes; live/film; 2 cameras; 1½ hours rehearsal; 4 hours preparation. Sponsored.

WEBSTER WEBFOOT SHOW. Webster Webfoot (an oversize duck puppet), the host, and ten children in the audience collaborate on the live portions of this program—jokes, games, songs, contests, stories with a moral, and courtesy and safety features, which also bring in members of Police and Fire Departments for interviews and safety hints. A weekly feature is animals and information on animals, provided by representatives of the Fresno Zoological Society. Scout, campfire, and school groups also appear for special events. Balance of program spent on cartoons. Age: preschool to 12. Monday through Friday; 1 hour; live/tape/film; 2 cameras; 1 hour rehearsal; 14 hours writing and preparation. Sponsored.

Grand Junction, Colorado

U.S. BANK CARTOON TIME. Host talks to studio children about their school, pets, etc., involves them in games and riddles, and lets them see themselves on monitor. Cartoons fill out the program. Age: 6 to 12. Wednesday evening; 30 minutes; 1 camera; live/film; 2 hours preparation; 30 minutes rehearsal.

Grand Rapids, Michigan

POPEYE THEATRE. The Monday-Wednesday-Friday host of this daily cartoon-based program dons fireman's costume to stress fire safety. The Tuesday-Thursday host works with the Humane Society to place lost and unclaimed dogs and gives tips on health and safety factors other than fire. Children participate as studio guests. Local government offices cooperate on production. Age: 6 to 12. Monday through Friday; 30 minutes; 2 cameras; live/tape/film; 30 minutes rehearsal; 1½ hours preparation. Sponsored.

Great Falls, Montana

PLAYTIME. Local information, patter and entertainment by host, informational film, cartoons, and instruction in arts and crafts. Simple set has lollipop tree on backdrop. Age: preschool to 9. Monday through Friday; 1 hour; live/film; 2 cameras; 2 hours preparation. Sponsored.

Green Bay, Wisconsin

SKIPPER SAM SHOW. Safety hints, puppet bits, sing-along records, and a variety of cartoons make up this program aboard the *Seagull*. Local civic and cultural organizations are occasionally represented as well as special creative groups from the schools. Age: 3 to 13. Monday through Friday; 25 minutes; live/film; 2 cameras; 1 hour rehearsal; 1 hour writing. Sponsored.

Greensboro, North Carolina

OLD REBEL AND PECOS PETE SHOW. Live portion devoted to public service announcements; locally produced films showing towns in coverage area and activities of Y and Scout groups; birthday children; drawing and other demonstrations. Basic set is interior of old mansion. Age: preschool to 9. Monday through Friday; 30 minutes; live/tape/film; 2 cameras; ½ hour rehearsal; 6½ hours preparation. Sponsored.

Harrisonburg, Virginia

CAPTAIN TREASURE. Host is captain of the ship *Bonnie Belle* and, with the assistance of his humorous sidekick, relates world-wide travels and experiences, natural wonders, weather facts, and subtle hints for living. Travel films, 35mm slide-and-script features, and cartoons are included. Children appear occasionally to show samples of their arts and crafts. Age: preschool to 12. Monday, Wednesday, and Friday; 30 minutes; live/film; 2 cameras; 45 minutes rehearsal; 2 hours writing and preparation. Sponsored.

Hartford, Connecticut

HAP RICHARDS SHOW. Setting of this program is a country store and post office in Joyville. To become a citizen of Joyville, a child writes a letter to the host telling of a good thing he has done "without being asked," for which he receives an appropriately inscribed certificate. The program is built around skits, puppet patter, music, a "smiling exercise," and educational films. Age: preschool. Monday through Friday; 15 minutes; tape/film; 2 cameras; 30 minutes rehearsal; 2 to 3 hours preparation. Sponsored.

RANGER ANDY SHOW. In a ranger station setting, the host leads studio children in a half-hour of games, songs, and riddles. Music and art teachers, museum curators, and persons with unusual occupations appear regularly to exhibit or demonstrate their crafts. An informational film is shown on each program. Age: preschool to 12. Monday through Friday; 30 minutes; 3 cameras; live/tape/film; 45 minutes rehearsal; 5 to 9 hours preparation. Sponsored.

Hattiesburg, Mississippi

ENGINEER BOB. Host interviews youngsters in a station-house setting, leads them in games, and instructs and entertains them with drawings. The Advertising Council, Illinois Central Railroad, Safety Council, and Scouts are among the film sources. Age: preschool to 9. Monday through Friday; 30 minutes; live/film; 2 cameras; 1 hour preparation. Sponsored.

Helena, Montana

CABLE THE CLOWN. In this ad-libbed program, the host interviews children, tells jokes and stories, and makes announcements while young participants play games, dance, and sing. Age: preschool to 9. Monday, Wednesday, and Thursday; 30 minutes; live; 2 cameras; 30 minutes rehearsal; 1 hour writing and preparation. Sponsored.

Houston, Texas

CADET DON. Host, operating from interior of space ship, conducts setting-up exercises, talks about safety and good citizenship, gives instructions in painting, and carries on with two space puppets, singing, extending birthday wishes, etc. Popular cartoons are integrated with live portions; civic groups send representatives as guests. Age: preschool to 12. Monday through Friday; 1½ hours (split: 6:30–7:30, 8:00–8:30 A.M.); live/tape/film; 3 cameras; 1 hour rehearsal; 3 hours writing and preparation. Sponsored.

KITIRIK'S CLUBHOUSE. A program of cartoons, with occasional instructional films from National Council of Churches, Safety Division of Police Department, or similar group. Hostess appears in costume of black cat in treehouse setting. Assisting her are two puppets and a live clown. They chatter along with Kitirik and listen to her suggestions on safety, children's books, and games. Age: preschool to 9. Monday through Friday; 40 minutes; tape/film; 4 cameras; 1 hour rehearsal; 6 hours preparation. Sponsored.

MR. CABOOSE, ENGINEER. From a stylized caboose on a railroad siding, a railroad clown (Mr. Caboose) and his puppet friend, Mr. Bookworm, try to operate a railroad, but their efforts are frequently frustrated. Serious vignettes dealing with holidays and history are frequently worked into the story line. Each program contains one cartoon; occasionally feature material from Pathé news film archives is used. Scouting groups, service clubs, PTA's, public officials cooperate in providing material. Age: preschool. Monday through Friday; early morning; 30 minutes; live/film. Sponsored.

TODAY IS SATURDAY. A "Today" program for children which includes a cartoon, an educational film, animal parade sequence (seeing-eye dogs, zoo babies), and perhaps a play or other demonstration put on by school children. Host and hostess also give a bit of news, drawing on films and resources of station news department. Age: 6 to 12. Saturdays; 1 hour; live/tape/film; 2 cameras.

Huntington, West Virginia

POPEYE AND HIS PALS. Puppet characters Popeye, Olive Oyl, Wimpy, and Swee'pea, aboard the *S.S. Spinach,* act out a different story each program; also give the children safety and health reminders. Cartoons shown between skit segments include Bugs Bunny, Popeye, and others. Age: preschool to 12. Saturdays; 1 hour; tape/film; 2 cameras; 1 hour rehearsal; 2 hours preparation. Sponsored.

STEAMBOAT BILL. Semidramatic story line adventures with Steamboat Bill and Merlin the sea monster, who have a kindly father—mischievous boy relationship. Their adventures take them down the river via a stern-wheeler, to the moon on a rocket ship, and back through history in a time machine. Cartoons are worked into the format. Age: preschool through junior high. Monday through Friday; 30 minutes; live/tape/film; 2 cameras; 1 hour rehearsal; 1½ hours writing and preparation. Sponsored.

Indianapolis, Indiana

ASSIGNMENT: TOMORROW and SCHOOL SHOWCASE. Excerpts from school plays, panel discussions, debates, and simulated classroom instruction show the schools in action. Locally prepared films are used occasionally. Students participate in the programs, and the schools' radio-television consultant arranges their appearance and prepares script. Indianapolis and Marion County school systems produce programs on alternate weeks. Age: 6 through high school. Saturdays; 30 minutes; live/film; 2 cameras; 2 hours rehearsal; 6 hours writing and preparation.

CURLEY'S COWBOY THEATRE. Host shows a 40-minute Western film and then plays the guitar and sings cowboy songs. Once a month the live portion is given over to an amateur show of local young performers. Age: 6 to 12. Saturday; 1 hour; live/film; 2 cameras; 1½ hours rehearsal, 5 hours preparation. Sponsored.

THE POPEYE SHOW. Interviews, local entertainment, specially written features on people and events in American history, and filmed tours through phone company, bottling plant, railroad switching yard, etc., alternate with Popeye, Felix, and Magoo cartoons. Public library, symphony orchestra and Armed Forces recruiters are regular contributors. Age: preschool to 12. Monday through Friday; 1¼ hours; live/tape/film; 3 cameras; 1 hour rehearsal; 4 hours preparation. Sponsored.

SELWIN ON SATURDAY. Host is a safari leader and the setting is his jungle hut. He appears in humorous skits, in which children also take part, and shows jungle movies. Indianapolis Zoological Society is associated with the program. Age: 6 to high school. Saturday afternoon; 1½ hours; tape/film; 2 cameras; 1 hour rehearsal; 6 hours writing and preparation. Sponsored.

FUN FAIR CIRCUS. Children take part in games, demonstrations, stunts, and contests and act in comedy situation episodes with the proprietor-host of a "fun fair circus." Film portions include cartoons, slapstick comedy, and madcap adventures of the host. City Park Department and Children's Theatre provide talent and material. Age: 6 to 12. Saturday morning; 1½ hours; live/tape/film; 2 cameras; 2 hours rehearsal; 14 hours writing and preparation. Sponsored.

Jackson, Mississippi

MIKE AND POPEYE. Popeye and Terrytoon cartoons presented before guest audience of 25 children. Mike, the host, interviews many of the children, paying special attention to birthdays. Brownies, Cubs, Little Leaguers often take over the bleachers. Age: preschool to 12. Monday through Friday; 1 hour; live/film; 2 cameras; 1 hour preparation. Sponsored.

Jacksonville, Florida

RANGER HAL. A forest ranger's outpost is the setting for this early morning variety program of exercises, stories, poems, nursery rhymes, art objects, and special features like a pet show and a bicycle rodeo. Children's Museum provides displays and background information. Age: preschool through 12. Monday through Saturday; 45 minutes; live/film; 2 cameras; 30 minutes rehearsal; 2 hours preparation. Sponsored.

Kalamazoo, Michigan

CHANNEL 3 CLUBHOUSE. Audience participation children's variety in a clubhouse set. Stunts, interviews with birthday children, entertainment films, and public service material are featured. Age: preschool through 12. Monday through Friday late afternoon; 30 minutes; live/film; 2 cameras; 30 minutes rehearsal; 2 hours writing and preparation. Sponsored.

Lansing, Michigan

RANGER JIM. A forest ranger and his puppet friends entertain and inform preschoolers in program of skits, songs about safety and manners, pets, films, and pen-pal correspondence, which provides geography lessons. Michigan State University Film Library and the Public Library cooperate on production. Age: preschool. Monday through Friday; 1 hour; live/film; 2 cameras; 1 hour rehearsal; 2 hours writing and preparation. Sponsored.

Lexington, Kentucky

WINDY WONDERFUL AND YOUNG PEOPLE'S WORLD. A puppet horse and its mistress offer interviews, cartoons, public service announcements, and educational films. Filmed portions are coordinated with grade schools. Age: preschool and up. Monday through Friday; 1 hour; live/film; 1 camera. Sponsored.

Lincoln, Nebraska

CARTOON THEATRE. Cartoons are spaced out with audience participation in games and demonstrations of talent, children's newscasts accompanied with maps and pictures, and slide/script material on weather and its causes. Age: preschool to 9. Monday through Friday; 1 hour; live/film; 2 cameras; 30 minutes rehearsal; 4½ hours writing and preparation. Sponsored.

Little Rock, Arkansas

MR. SPECS' CARTOON CARAVAN. Bespectacled host in cutaway and top hat entertains audience with comedy sketches (using puppets), riddles, stories, practical jokes, marching, exercises, demonstrations. He also shows drawings and reads letters sent in by children. Once a week he takes them on a trip (via magic balloon and film) to a foreign land. He also shows educational films from Encyclopaedia Britannica and popular cartoons. Exterior and interior of gingerbread house alternate as sets; house is crammed with toys. Age: preschool. Monday through Friday; 1 hour; live/film; 2 cameras; 1 hour preparation. Sponsored.

Los Angeles, California *

BOZO THE CLOWN. Originated in Los Angeles in 1957, this program combines a local personality, dressed and made up as a clown, with 6-minute syndicated cartoon adventures of Bozo. National syndicator provides costumes, production suggestions, and routines; training at Los Angeles studios is available for the local actor or announcer taking role of Bozo. Children usually participate in the program in games, health and safety hints, magic tricks, and other live entertainment. In many communities, Bozo has become a leading figure in promoting community public service activities. Age: preschool to 12. Usually Monday through Friday late afternoon; half-hour, 45 minutes, or one hour; live/film; 2 cameras; 2 to 10 hours preparation. Usually sponsored.

* Local productions also reported from Birmingham, Alabama; Fort Wayne, Indiana; Bangor, Maine; Baltimore, Maryland; Boston, Massachusetts; Minneapolis, Minnesota; Omaha, Nebraska; Utica, New York; Greenville and Raleigh, North Carolina; La Crosse, Wisconsin.

CHUCKO THE CLOWN. Children take part in games, stunts, jokes, drawing instructions, and scientific experiments. Cartoons and informational films furnished by local industries and public service organizations are shown. Aerojet, Marineland, and local zoo and animal shelters participate in production. Age: preschool to 12. Monday through Friday; 1 hour; live/film; 2 cameras; 18 hours preparation. Sponsored.

NORTH POLE REVUE. Santa Claus is star of this program, which spans late fall and winter. With assistance of his major domo, he tells of Christmas in many lands, reads good-deed letters, cautions children on safety, plays records, and tells stories. In his office at North Pole he also keeps white book inscribed with names of good girls and boys. Age: preschool. Monday through Friday; 30 minutes; live/film; 1 camera; 1 hour rehearsal; 3 hours writing and preparation. Sponsored.

PANORAMA PACIFIC. A morning variety program that has segments directed to preschool and elementary school children—a weekly spot about the zoo, visits and interviews with cub scouts and other young groups, an "exercise lady" who works with youngsters and adults, a trip to Marineland. Age: preschool to adult. Monday through Friday; 1 hour; live/film.

POPEYE. Popeye and other cartoons are integrated with live portions in which children participate. They include a "squiggle" contest, in which three children compete in making a picture with a prize going to the winner; interviews, games, and quizzes. Age: 2 to 14. Monday through Friday; 1 hour; live/tape/film; 2 cameras; 4 hours preparation. Sponsored.

SKIPPER FRANK'S CARTOON CAROUSEL. Host entertains guest children with games, magic, contests and interviews in his ship setting, and shows entertainment cartoons. Age: 2 to 14. Monday through Friday afternoon; 1½ hours; live/tape/film; 2 cameras; 4 hours preparation. Sponsored.

THE SOUPY SALES SHOW. Comedian and puppets perform in classic slapstick comedy situations, often ending with a pie in the face. Age: preschool and up. Monday through Friday late afternoon; 30 minutes; live; 2 cameras; 23 hours writing and preparation. Sponsored.

Louisville, Kentucky

HI VARIETIES. Talent show presented by teenagers and ranging from individuals and small groups to school bands and choruses. The program is used frequently in fund-raising campaigns. Local school, college, and public service groups assist in production. Age: entire family. Saturday; 1 hour; live/tape; 2 cameras; 3 hours rehearsal; 19 hours preparation. Sponsored.

POPEYE'S ADVENTURES. Host holds conversations with live parrot by means of prerecorded voice and refers questions to it (written in by viewers) which the parrot answers. The live portions are wrapped around Popeye cartoons. Age: 6 to 12. Monday though Friday; 45 minutes; tape/film; 2 cameras; 3½ hours writing and preparation. Sponsored.

T-BAR-V RANCH. Variety program in a ranch-house setting with interviews, songs, safety instructions, slides, stories, and educational films. Services of the library and city departments are used in programming. Age: preschool. Monday through Friday; 45 minutes; live/tape/film; 2 cameras; 3¼ hours preparation. Sponsored.

Madison, Wisconsin

THIS CURIOUS WORLD. Host interviews guests who are experts or outstanding men and women in their field. Informational films are also shown. Setting backdrop is a world map. Age: teens. Saturday afternoon; 30 minutes; live/film; 1 camera; 1 hour rehearsal; 5 hours preparation.

Mason City, Iowa

BART'S CLUBHOUSE. Program of games, puppets, record pantomimes, films, storytelling, craft instruction, suggestions on safety and etiquette, and pets in need of homes. An "Irish Leprechaun" is a regular guest (special shot reduces his height to one foot). Setting is a clubhouse interior. Age: preschool to 12. Monday through Friday; 45 minutes; live/film; 2 cameras; 2 or more hours writing and preparation. Sponsored.

Marquette, Michigan

DARBY O'SIX AND THE LITTLE PEOPLE. Varied format of puppets, games, informational films, cartoons, drawing instruction, and facts on science and history. Children participate occasionally to show their handicrafts or put on skits. Local PTA and American Association of University Women request time on program to promote charity events and present educational segments. Age: preschool to 12. Monday through Friday; 45 minutes; live/film; 2 cameras; 2 hours rehearsal; 6 to 8 hours preparation. Sponsored.

Memphis, Tennessee

LOONEY ZOO. Interviews with children, play excerpts from the Children's Theatre, informational films, cartoons, and clown and puppet patter. Setting is a combined circus and zoo. Art gallery, museum, and Kiwanis are among cooperating groups. Age: preschool to 12. Monday through Friday; 1 hour; live/film; 2 cameras; 30 minutes rehearsal; 8 hours writing and preparation. Sponsored.

Miami, Florida

BANJO BILLY'S FUNBOAT. Continuous story-line adventures of a showboat captain and his friends on the river. Host sings, draws, works with puppets, and shows cartoons. Children play games and act in "play theatre" sketches. Humane Society of Miami shows pets available for adoption and gives tips on animal care. Age: preschool. Monday through Friday; 1 hour; live/film; 2 cameras; 5 hours writing and preparation. Sponsored.

BANJO BILLY'S PALS. Children sing, play games, and watch puppets and marionettes perform. Setting is a riverfront pier with showboat. Cartoons vary the format. Age: 6 to 9. Monday through Friday; 30 minutes; live/film; 2 cameras; 30 minutes rehearsal; 5 hours writing and preparation. Sponsored.

FUN CLUB. Twelve children participate each week in a program of games, stunts, and instructions. Cartoons are shown to space out the hour. Age: preschool to 9. Saturday; 1 hour; live/tape/film; 2 cameras; 2 to 3 hours rehearsal; 18 to 23 hours preparation. Sponsored.

MARY JANE AND MELVIN. An audience participation program interspersed with cartoons. Young guests receive small gifts (coloring books, clown hat, membership cards, etc.) and take part in exercises, birthday celebrations, games, marches. Outdoor garden set allows ample room for Melvin, a giant giraffe; children sit on grass mats and benches. Local Humane Society appears every other week with animal for adoption or unusual animal for viewing. Age: preschool. Sundays; 30 minutes; live/film; 2 cameras; 30 minutes rehearsal; 1 hour preparation. Sponsored.

Milwaukee, Wisconsin

CARTOON ALLEY. Hostess and eight animal puppets act out entertaining and informative stories. Children occasionally join hostess and puppets to sing simple songs. Cartoons are integrated with live portions. Monday through Friday, 30 minutes; Saturday, 1 hour; live/film.

WEE WEEKLY. A program of puppet plays, safety stories and dramatizations, craft lessons, hobbies, pets, and interviews set in the offices of a safety newspaper. Children appear occasionally as guests. Milwaukee Institute of Technology, library, Police and Fire Departments and Safety Commission participate in production. Age: 6 to 9. Friday late afternoon; 30 minutes; live/tape; 2 cameras; 2 hours rehearsal; 8 hours writing and preparation.

Minneapolis, Minnesota

LUNCH WITH CASEY. The depot or the cab of Engine 11 is the setting; cartoons, Encyclopaedia Britannica films, games, jokes, ice-skating instructions, make up the bill of fare at lunch with Casey. Age: 6 to 9. Monday through Friday; 1 hour; live/tape/film; 2 cameras; 30 minutes rehearsal; 2 hours preparation. Sponsored.

POPEYE AND PETE, WITH DAVE LEE. The adventures of a collection of hand puppets—Fragrant the Skunk, Omar the Alligator, and so on—are recounted by host before studio audience of 30 children. Puppets also interview the youngsters and periodically retire backstage for Popeye, Felix, and other cartoons. Age: preschool to 9. Monday through Friday; 45 minutes; live/film; 2 cameras; 1 hour rehearsal; 1½ hours preparation. Sponsored.

T. N. TATTERS. Host leads studio children in games and contests, tells jokes, and shows entertainment films. Age: preschool to 12. Monday through Friday afternoon; 45 minutes; live/film; 2 cameras; 30 minutes rehearsal; 5½ hours preparation. Sponsored.

Mobile, Alabama

BUNNYVILLE, U.S.A. Host Barney Bunny, in costume of a rabbit, presents a program of cartoons with live bits during which he tries to be a magician, but fails. Age: preschool to 10. Saturdays; 30 minutes; live/film; 1 camera.

CAPTAIN MAL'S FRIENDS. Friends of the host are a puppet, Birdie, and a hostess, Miss Beverly, who contribute to live portions with patter about local events of interest to children. Between cartoons, host gives drawing lessons. Age: 6 to 12. Monday through Friday, 1½ hours; Saturdays, 30 minutes; live/film; 1 camera. Sponsored.

CARTOONERVILLE. Chuck Wagon Charlie, with four or five young guests, conducts a program of cartoons from an old country store. During live sequences he interviews the children, tells stories, and reads the mail. Another member of station staff presents puppet skits. Occasional guests of interest to audience are fire chief, storyteller, or person skilled in arts and crafts. Age: preschool. Monday through Friday; 30 minutes; live/film; 1 camera.

THE POPEYE CARTOON THEATRE. As skipper of the *S.S. Popeye*, Captain Hank makes his young audience feel at home with interviews, jokes, and patter; magic tricks, birthday celebrations, and animal and other guests. He also awards prizes every day and occasionally conducts big contests. Additional live features are added for special events, such as Christmas. An average of three Popeye cartoons are shown each time. Age: preschool to 12. Monday through Friday; 30 minutes; live/film; 2 cameras.

Monroe, Louisiana

HAPPINESS EXCHANGE. Variety program before a studio audience of 450 children and parents. Performers include teen-age pupils of local dancing schools and younger children who participate extemporaneously. Interviews with special guests, a party for birthday children, and a cartoon are included on each program. Age: preschool through teens. Saturday; 1 hour; live/film; 2 cameras; 1½ hours rehearsal; 16 hours preparation. Sponsored.

Montgomery, Alabama

POPEYE THEATRE. Skipper host entertains children on shipboard set, leads songs and dances, shows Popeye cartoons. Age: 4 to 12. Monday through Friday; 30 minutes; live/film; 2 cameras; 1 hour preparation. Sponsored.

Nashville, Tennessee

HAPPY TOWN GANG. Mayor of Happy Town presides over a program of live entertainment, cartoons, and visits to the editor of the *Happy Town Bugle*, who illustrates the news with selections from educational films. Setting shows different buildings and streets in Happy Town. Age: 6 to 12. Monday through Friday; 1 hour; live/tape/film; 2 cameras. Sponsored.

New Britain, Connecticut

COLONEL CLOWN SHOW. A completely live program presented before a live audience of 20 or so children. Pledge of allegiance, spelling bees, games ("Simon Says"), songs and prayers, instructional bits on manners and health, are among regular features. Age: 3 to 12. Saturdays; 30 minutes; live.

New Haven, Connecticut

BREAKFAST TIME WITH HAPPY THE CLOWN. Children join clown host in a lengthy morning program of songs, games, puppet skits (always keyed to topical events such as elections), and demonstrations of hobbies, arts, crafts, and talented pets. Cartoons are also used. Age: preschool to 12. Monday through Friday; 1½ hours; live/tape/film; 2 cameras; 3 hours rehearsal; 12 to 14 hours writing and preparation. Sponsored.

POPEYE THEATRE. Program's host supplements 30 minutes of cartoons with patter, informational features such as "Know Your America" and "Know Your Connecticut," and live sequences in which children display their hobbies and pets. Age: 6 to 12. Monday through Friday; 55 minutes; live/tape/film; 2 cameras; 2½ hours rehearsal; 14 hours preparation. Sponsored.

New Orleans, Louisiana

GOOD OLD BOB DREWS. A program of entertainment and interviews with the studio audience. The host introduces a variety of characters, real and invisible, to his audience, including the engineer of a model railroad featured on the program. Cartoons space out the hour. Age: preschool. Monday through Friday; 1 hour; live/film; 2 cameras; 30 minutes rehearsal; 1 hour writing and preparation. Sponsored.

New York, New York

AMERICAN TREASURE CHEST. Host tells stories and leads the children in the audience in songs and games. All activities are related to educational theme of program. Age: preschool to 9. Saturdays; 30 minutes; tape; 3 cameras; 1 hour rehearsal; 8 hours writing and preparation.

JUST FOR FUN. Two teams of fifty children compete for prizes in games and stunts based on skill and physical ingenuity—for example: matching animals with animal tracks, passing a plate with their laps, catching a 45-rpm record on the end of a pole. A half-hour of cartoons are shown during program. Many organizations are associated with production: Boy and Girl Scouts, Boys Club of New York, Police and Fire Departments, Visiting Nurse Service, Olympic Fencing Team. All groups help in setting up stunts in which their organizations participate. Two large bleachers, erected on either side of stunt area, provide set. Age: 10 to 12. Saturdays; 2½ hours; tape/film; 3 cameras; 12 hours rehearsal; 120 hours preparation. Sponsored.

SANDY'S HOUR. The host, an experienced actor, entertains and instructs children through pantomime, characterizations, and puppetry. Two of his characters are the "answer men" who reply to questions sent in by viewers. Cartoons are also shown. Age: preschool to 12. Monday through Friday; 1 hour; live/tape/film; 2 cameras; 20 hours rehearsal; 25 hours writing and preparation. Sponsored.

Norfolk, Virginia

BUNGLES AND HIS FRIENDS. Clown-host Bungles and a collection of his off-beat friends are responsible for live portions of this program, which consist of dancing, singing, art contests, guessing games, and tips on health habits, dress, and manners. Two sets are used—a rumpus room and a small stage area for puppets. Cartoons are shown. Age: 6 to 12. Monday through Friday; 50 minutes; live/tape/film; 2 cameras; 2 hours preparation. Sponsored.

Omaha, Nebraska

TALENT SHOWCASE. Area children demonstrate their various talents. The station auditions all youngsters who wish to perform on the program. Age: 6 to 12. Saturday; 30 minutes; live/tape; 2 cameras; 2 hours rehearsal; 2 hours writing and preparation.

Onondaga, Michigan

TAMS FUN TIME. Children play games with host and watch cartoons. Scout and Savings Bonds campaigns are promoted. Age: preschool to 9. Saturday morning; 30 minutes; 2 cameras; live/film; 20 hours preparation.

Orlando, Florida

CARTOONVILLE. Puppet conversation about current events, birthday announcements, and answers to questions sent in by viewers augment cartoon portions of the program. The puppets perform in three settings—a soda shop, a missile control room, and on the street. Age: preschool; all ages Saturday. Monday through Friday, 1¼ hours; Saturday, 1½ hours; live/tape/film; 2 cameras; 1 hour rehearsal; 1 hour preparation. Sponsored.

UNCLE WALT'S ADVENTURES IN TIME AND SPACE. A program of entertainment and information conducted in a simulated rocket-launching site blockhouse. Space Quiz is conducted regularly, and the program is planning a model rocket shoot to point up correct conditions for a shoot and the danger involved in firing homemade rockets. Content departs from space theme to stress safety, good behavior, treatment of animals, and respect for authority. Informational films are used occasionally. Age: 3 to 14. Monday through Friday; 30 minutes; live/film; 2 cameras. Sponsored.

Parkersburg, West Virginia

FUN CLUB. Hostess presides over a program of games, projects, and story-telling interspersed with cartoons. Age: preschool to 12. Monday through Friday; 1 hour; live/film; 1 camera; 3 to 8 hours preparation. Sponsored.

Philadelphia, Pennsylvania

HAPPY THE CLOWN SHOW. With the assistance of a dozen or so children each day, the clown-host builds a program of creative play, puppetry, stories, songs, and discussions of the news and weather, balanced with cartoons. Setting is a train depot and observation platform of the Happyland Express. Age: preschool to 9. Monday through Friday; 1 hour; live/tape/film; 3 cameras; 2 hours rehearsal; 18 to 21 hours preparation. Sponsored.

PETE'S GANG. An audience participation program in which young guests exhibit their hobbies and collections, joke with the host, and are entertained by his drawings and patter. An occasional film or cartoon may be shown; when it is, host relates his drawings and banter to subject matter. "Kids' Clubhouse" is setting. Age: preschool to 12. Saturdays and Sundays; 1 hour; tape/film; 1 hour rehearsal; 3 to 4 hours preparation. Sponsored.

PIXANNE SHOW. Pixanne and her friends, real and puppet, live in an enchanted forest, which provides setting for continuous story line. (In one segment, for example, Windy Witch—a good witch—sorrowfully decides she must abandon her witchery because of the bad reputation witches have.) Original songs are integrated in plot. Program also features cartoons and educational films and a specially prepared news segment for children that is supplemented by film clips and stills. Philadelphia Zoo, Dance Academy, and SPCA are actively associated with production. Child guests—on Saturdays only—become part of the program's story plot. Age: preschool to 9. Monday through Friday, 15 minutes; Saturday, 30 minutes; live/tape/film; 2 cameras; 1 hour rehearsal; 5 hours writing and preparation. Sponsored.

Phoenix, Arizona

IT'S WALLACE. Format of cartoons and comedy routines is vehicle for Wallace and his sidekick, Ladmo. Drawing from current events and local and national personalities in the news, they build program of comedy and satire which may be live or filmed out of doors. "Name" guests appear frequently. Age: 6 to 18. Monday through Friday; 1 hour; live/tape/film; 2 cameras; 1 hour rehearsal; 8 hours preparation. Sponsored.

SHERIFF BILL. Host on this daily two-hour program is a bona fide fast-draw fire artist. With the assistance of studio children, he gives lessons on safety, Arizona wildlife, desert survival, Southwest history, Indian craft and lore, and care and feeding of pets. He also talks with guests on civic responsibility and the child's role in the total family picture. Setting is the sheriff's office with desk, jail cells, notices, and gun rack. City, county, and state police departments cooperate on production. Age: 6 to 12. Monday through Friday afternoon; 2 hours; live/tape/film; 2 cameras; 9 hours rehearsal; 7 hours writing and preparation. Sponsored.

Pittsburgh, Pennsylvania

ADVENTURE TIME. Host presents a program of cartoons for a studio audience of local scout groups. The children sing songs in live segments. Setting is a game room. Age: 6 to 16. Monday through Friday; 1¼ hours; live/film; 2 cameras; 2 hours rehearsal; 4 hours preparation. Sponsored.

FUNSVILLE. A group of puppets inhabit the fanciful town of Funsville and have experiences with its talking train and haunted house, as well as with some of the inhabitants of the town. Funsville provides the background for puppet skits, simple craft lessons, songs, and cartoons, all presided over by a hostess. She is assisted by a variety of characters who alternate puppet segments with jokes, patter, songs, and cartoons. Children participate frequently. Basic set is impressionistic exterior of town; various other sets serve as vehicles for characters. Carnegie Library, associated with production, promotes books of special interest to the audience. Age: 6 to 14. Monday through Friday; 30 minutes; live/film; 2 cameras; 30 minutes rehearsal; 7 hours preparation. Sponsored.

MORNING IN FUNSVILLE. The Funsville set and characters adapted to a morning audience of preschoolers and their mothers. Age: preschool. Monday through Friday; 30 minutes; live/film; 2 cameras; 30 minutes rehearsal; 6 hours writing and preparation. Sponsored.

Ricki and copper. Hostess and her Irish setter entertain studio children in a program that includes songs, stories, magic, and cartoons. Set is a wooded fairyland. Age: preschool. Monday through Friday; 30 minutes; live/film; 2 cameras; 1 hour rehearsal; 5 hours preparation. Sponsored.

Portland, Maine

The cap'n and the kids. In a waterfront setting with fish net, wharf pilings, and lobster traps, the host entertains youngsters with songs, music, stories, and cartoons. Age: preschool to 9. Monday through Friday; 30 minutes; live/film; 2 cameras; 15 minutes rehearsal; 4 hours preparation. Sponsored.

Teddy bear playhouse. Hostess and teddy bear friends build a program of puppetry, crayon-paper-scissors projects, stories, and poetry. Viewers submit photos and enter coloring and guessing contests. Cartoons and educational films are included. State Teachers Association contributes to programming. Age: preschool to 9. Monday through Saturday morning; 1½ hours; live/film; 2 cameras; 1 hour rehearsal; 3 to 4 hours preparation. Sponsored.

Portland, Oregon

Cartoon circus. In live portions between cartoons, host interviews Scouts and Camp Fire Girls, greets birthday children, and jokes with studio audience. Animals, circus personalities, and magicians highlight circus atmosphere. Age: preschool to 9. Monday through Friday; 30 minutes; live/film; 2 cameras; 30 minutes rehearsal; 2 hours preparation. Sponsored.

Providence, Rhode Island

Salty's shack. Salty, the host, takes children on filmed visits to the nearby lighthouse, whaling museum, and fire-engine factory. Children appear on the program to exhibit school projects. Other features are bicycle safety, animals and plants, puppets in pantomime to music, films and cartoons. Age: preschool to 12. Monday through Friday; 1 hour; live/film; 2 cameras; 30 minutes rehearsal; 1 hour preparation. Sponsored.

Raleigh, North Carolina

Captain 5 show. Puppet acts, interviews with children, and patter alternate with cartoons. Age: preschool to 9. Monday through Friday; 1 hour; live/tape/film; 2 cameras; 2 hours preparation. Sponsored.

Richmond, Virginia

Popeye and friends. Sailor Bob is the host of this cartoon program, which he supplements with puppet patter, drawing instructions on camera, drawing to music, daily reading of the birthday log, and special guests promoting civic and educational activities. Station-produced film and tape material and Encyclopaedia Britannica films are integrated with the Popeye cartoons. Women's Club, Junior Chamber of Commerce, and other groups are associated with production. Age: preschool to 12. Monday through Friday; 25 minutes in morning, 40 minutes in late afternoon; live/tape/film; 1½ hours rehearsal; 5½ hours preparation. Sponsored.

Sacramento, California

DIVER DAN'S TREASURE CHEST. Live portions in this morning cartoon program include jokes, riddles, songs, patter, school announcements, safety tips, and community news. Two sets: interior and outside of a tugboat. Two elementary school teachers advise on programming. Age: preschool to 9. Monday through Friday, 1½ hours; Saturday, 30 minutes; tape/film; 2 cameras; 1 to 2 hours rehearsal; 6 to 7 hours preparation. Sponsored.

O. U. SQUID SHOW. An octopus and a fish puppet share the live portion of this program with jokes, riddles, and announcements of community activities for children. Underwater scene of sunken boat is setting; puppet segments are shot through fish bowl stocked with live guppies. Cartoons and films also shown. Age: preschool. Sundays; 30 minutes; tape/film; 2 cameras; 1 to 2 hours rehearsal; 8 hours writing and preparation. Sponsored.

St. Louis, Missouri

CHARLOTTE PETERS SHOW. During a daily segment of this women's noontime program, hostess reads stories, shows children how to make greeting cards, and gives safety suggestions. Age: 4 to 12. Monday through Friday; live/tape; 2 cameras. Sponsored.

CORKY THE CLOWN. Clown host in a circus setting presides over a program of drawing lessons, birthday announcements, animal games, riddles, and cartoons. Age: 4 to 12. Saturday morning; 30 minutes; tape/film; 2 cameras; 1 hour rehearsal; 6 hours preparation. Sponsored.

LORENZO AND FRIENDS. Host appears between cartoons in guise of tramp, poet, or storyteller to tell tall tales of the Old West or perform in a music or comedy skit with wind-up toys, tropical fish, and a magic window for line drawings. Age: preschool. Monday through Friday; 1 hour; live/tape/film; 2 cameras; 2 hours rehearsal; 7½ hours preparation. Sponsored.

S.S. POPEYE WITH COOKY AND THE CAPTAIN. With children participating as cabin mates, Cooky and the Captain act out situation comedy routines. They promote safety and good citizenship through the use of special films made on location in the city. Popeye and Dick Tracy cartoons are included. Age: preschool to 9. Monday through Friday, 30 minutes; Saturday, 1 hour; live/ tape/film; 2 cameras; 1 hour preparation; 1 hour rehearsal. Sponsored.

SUZY'S PLAYROOM. The 10-year-old mistress of the playroom conducts her program before studio audience of 50 children. Suzy shows winners in drawing contest, turns on her "television set" to a puppet performance, and gives her own commercials. Cartoons and information films fill out the program. Age: 5 to 13. Saturday; 30 minutes; live/tape/film; 2 cameras; 8 hours rehearsal; 10 hours preparation. Sponsored.

THE WORLD OF MR. ZOOM AND NEWS FOR CHILDREN. The puppeteer and magician host leads his entourage of puppets in a medieval castle setting. Hostess reads news and supplements items with pictures and news film. Cartoons are interspersed. Age: preschool to 9. Monday through Friday; 20 minutes; live/film; 2 cameras; 1 or more hours rehearsal. Sponsored.

WHISTLE V RANCH. Host gives short lessons in border Spanish, and relates western lore about guns, arrows, and saddles. Cartoons are included. Local school groups help. Age: 4 to 12. Saturday; 30 minutes; live/tape/film; 2 cameras; 1 hour rehearsal; 8 hours writing and preparation. Sponsored.

San Diego, California

JOHNNY DOWNS SHOW. A program of films and cartoons before live studio audience. Children are invited to exhibit hobbies and join in games. Cub scouts and other groups often appear in body. Age: preschool to 12. Monday through Friday; 30 minutes; live/film; 2 cameras; 30 minutes rehearsal; 2 hours preparation. Sponsored.

POPEYE. Captain's cabin is setting for this program of Popeye cartoons, games, and patter by host. Children in audience are interviewed and also demonstrate their hobbies. Age: preschool to 12. Monday through Friday; 30 minutes; live/film; 2 cameras; 2 hours preparation. Sponsored.

San Francisco, California

FUN HOUSE. In a family room setting, the puppeteer host and six children present a program of cartoons, puppet show, and interviews. Children decorate the Fun House on holidays and the host explains the historical significance of the event. The program conducts a snapshot contest with simple instructions on photography and awards to the winners. Age: 4 to 11. Monday, Tuesday, Thursday, and Friday; 30 minutes; live/tape/film; 2 cameras; 30 minutes rehearsal; 6 to 8 hours preparation. Sponsored.

POPEYE SHOW WITH MAYOR ART. On live portions of this cartoon program, the host presents a children's newscast supported with maps and pictures, teaches a foreign word or phrase each day, and gives health and safety tips. Setting is an old general store. Newspaper, zoo, and science academy contribute material. Age: 6 to 12. Monday through Friday; 1 hour; live/tape/film; 2 cameras; 2¼ hours rehearsal; 9 hours preparation. Sponsored.

Schenectady, New York

BREADTIME STORIES. Host, an artist and designer, entertains studio audience with stories, games, and cartoons drawn on the air. In a "squiggle" segment, children draw lines or a design which the host develops into a cartoon. He tells animal stories and illustrates them with cartoons drawn on the spot. Age: preschool to 9. Monday through Friday; 15 minutes; live/film; 2 cameras; 30 minutes rehearsal; 4 hours writing and preparation. Sponsored.

Scranton, Pennsylvania

HATCHY MILATCHY. Two-hour variety program including daily calendar, birthday mail, health tips, drawing and coloring assignments, shots of classroom scenes, cartoons, and educational films. Fanciful setting of personalized objects (smiling alarm clock, giant piggy bank) against a fairy-tale backdrop. Age: preschool. Monday through Friday; 2 hours; live/film; 2 cameras; 1½ hours rehearsal; 5 hours preparation. Sponsored.

MAGIC WINDOW. Cartoon program held together by conversation, instructions, and puppet skits. Children appear as occasional guests and are urged to participate at home in drawings and other projects. Scouts and church groups prepare scrapbooks for sick children. Weather Bureau, Traffic Safety (Police Department), and other civic organizations participate. Age: preschool. Monday through Friday; 30 minutes; live/film; 2 cameras; 1 hour rehearsal; 10 hours preparation. Sponsored.

UNCLE TED. A program of talk, games, interviews, puppets, music, singing, dancing, and cartoons presented in a carnival setting. Children appear as guests and amateur performers. Scouting and church organizations cooperate on production. Age: 6 to 9. Sunday; 30 minutes; 2 cameras; live/film; 1 hour rehearsal; 8 hours preparation. Sponsored.

Seattle, Washington

CAPTAIN PUGET. Host, a skin diver and yachtsman, conducts this program of interviews, cartoons, and informational films (for which the sound track is rewritten and voiced by host). Portions of local plays for children and presentations of young talent are included in live portions. Conservation and sports groups cooperate. Age: 8 to 14. Monday through Friday; 30 minutes; live/film; 2 cameras; 8 or more hours writing and preparation.

J. P. PATCHES. In a shack down by the city dump, Patches, a retired clown, entertains a young television audience with skits, patter, cartoons, and live animal guests; he also shows station-filmed newsreels of school and group activities. Representatives of civic organizations are regular guests. Age: 6 to 12. Monday through Friday; 45 minutes; live/tape/film; 2 cameras; 2 to 2½ hours rehearsal; 1½ to 2 hours preparation. Sponsored.

WUNDA WUNDA. Puppet program presided over by hostess Wunda Wunda, whose "friends" enjoy songs, speech games, and mild bits of instruction on manners, attitudes, and so on; they also act out the daily puppet sequences that are integrated with program. About eight minutes of program set aside for story; once a week is "travel day," and then hostess takes off on magic carpet and tells story set in another land or long ago in the United States. Authentic visual and musical effects produced through use of miniature sets, museum pieces, and recordings. Age: preschool. Monday through Friday, 30 minutes, Seattle; taped for Portland showing Saturday and Sunday, 1 hour; live; 2 to 3 cameras; 2 hours rehearsal; 8 hours writing and preparation. Sponsored.

Shreveport, Louisiana

CLYDE AND SAM'S POPEYE CARTOON SPECTACULAR. Host and two puppets present a program of cartoons and informational films. Age: preschool to 9. Saturday; 1 hour; tape/film; 1 camera; 2 hours preparation. Sponsored.

Sioux City, Iowa

KIDS' KORNER. With about 15 children in attendance, host talks briefly about safety, shows pictures they have submitted, sends off birthday greetings, interviews guests of interest to children and also the children themselves. Ten- to twelve-minute segment each day is set aside for special feature. Monday: local librarian tells and illustrates story; Tuesday: children's pets are performers; Wednesday: staff artists give drawing lesson and draw picture for children to copy and compete for prize; Thursday: child talent exhibited; Friday: host takes viewers on filmed tour of local point of interest —museum, dam, firehouse, factory. Age: preschool to 12. Monday through Friday; 25 minutes; live/film; 2 cameras; 8 hours preparation. Sponsored.

Sioux Falls, South Dakota

CAPTAIN ELEVEN. Cartoons alternate with simple scientific demonstrations, interviews with celebrities and out-of-town children, and birthday and get-well wishes. Hospital and charitable organizations cooperate. Age: preschool to 9. Monday through Friday; 1¼ hours; live/tape/film; 4 cameras; 1 hour rehearsal; 2 hours preparation. Sponsored.

South Bend, Indiana

KIDSVILLE USA. Large canine puppet is mayor of Kidsville. With other puppet friends he dramatizes "cliff-hanger" stories written by host, appears in humorous sketches, tells jokes, reports weather news. Balance of program consists of cartoons and films. Cub scouts and other groups are occasional guests. Age: 6 to 12. Monday through Friday; 30 minutes; tape/film; 2 cameras; 1 hour rehearsal; 3 hours writing and preparation. Sponsored.

POPEYE THEATRE. Host and his puppets interview children in studio audience, read from the birthday book, and show about six cartoons per program. Weekly feature, "Junior Newsroom," prepared in cooperation with elementary school teachers, keeps children up to date on current events. Monday through Friday; 1 hour; live/film.

Spokane, Washington

BAR 6 ROUNDUP. A singing cowboy and his pony, Little Bit, in format that combines songs, talk, and cartoons. Children in audience sing along with host, participate in games, are interviewed. Western set, with corral for horse. Age: 5 to 12. Monday through Friday; 30 minutes; live/film; 2 cameras; 2½ hours rehearsal.

MR. WALLABY AND JACK. Mr. Wallaby, a kangaroo, is star of this program, which combines cartoons with live sequences in which audience participates —e.g., dances (Wallaby hop), games (musical chairs, pin the tail on the donkey), demonstrations by local schools, and interviews. Host also makes public service and safety announcements. Age: preschool to 12. Monday through Friday; 1 hour; live/film; 2 cameras; 30 minutes rehearsal; 3 or more hours writing and preparation. Sponsored.

Springfield, Illinois

BUGS BUNNY AND HIS PEGWILL PALS WITH CLICKA T. CLACK. Program host is conductor of the Bugs Bunny Express which daily discharges its cargo of cartoons. Studio guests join host in singing songs and talking about their hobbies and interesting places nearby to visit. Age: preschool to 9. Monday through Friday; 30 minutes; live/film; 2 cameras; 30 minutes rehearsal; 30 minutes preparation. Sponsored.

137

Springfield, Massachusetts

ADMIRAL AND SWABBY. Comedy sketches, live animals from local zoo, books, science, safety, and space travel are the subjects of this late-afternoon program. Age: preschool to 12. Monday through Friday; 30 minutes; live/film; 2 cameras; 1 hour rehearsal; 2 hours writing and preparation. Sponsored.

Tacoma, Washington

PENNY AND HER PALS. Penny is a ventriloquist who entertains the studio audience with the doings of her big and little pals, and with cartoons. Brownie, Bluebird, or Cub scout groups are guests each week. Age: preschool to 9. Monday through Friday; 1 hour; live/film; 1 camera. Sponsored.

Tallahassee, Florida

CIRCLE SIX RANCH. Cowboy host in a western setting interviews children and entertains them with cartoons, drawing lessons, live animals, riddles, and educational slides. Age: preschool to 12. Monday through Friday; 30 minutes; live/tape/film; 2 cameras; 1 hour preparation. Sponsored.

Tampa, Florida

KID'S CAROUSEL. Program host, an ordained minister, uses his talents as ventriloquist and puppeteer to entertain studio audience. Children also participate in games and watch antics of live clown and science chalk talk by staff scientist. Mr. Magoo and other cartoons are shown. Regularly recurring features are Dogland (interviews concerning pedigreed dogs), contests, and visits from representatives of school system. Age: preschool to 9. Monday through Friday; 30 minutes; live/tape/film; 2 cameras; 10 hours writing and preparation. Sponsored.

THE MARY ELLEN SHOW. Hostess enlivens live portions of program with her talents as cartoonist; also draws studio audience into games, contests, and interviews. Popeye, Bozo, Dick Tracy, and other cartoons are shown. Children guests sit on chairs or pillows. Age: preschool to 12. Monday through Friday, 30 minutes; Saturdays, 1 hour; live/film; 2 cameras. Sponsored.

Toledo, Ohio

CAPTAIN COTTON AND SALTY. Comedy and adventure situations involving a riverboat captain, his first mate, and other characters in the wheelhouse of a riverboat setting. The program also includes interviews, animal guests, and news for children. Age: preschool to 9. Monday through Friday; 1 hour; live/film; 2 cameras; 2½ hours rehearsal; 11 hours writing and preparation.

Topeka, Kansas

KRAKO'S KOMEDY KLUB. Clown host entertains live audience in circus setting, interviewing young guests, reading mail, presenting birthday wishes. Cartoons are interspersed with program's other features—dance group, Bible story, safety instruction. Many civic and educational organizations are associated with production—Police and Fire Departments, dance studios, Council of Churches. Age: preschool to 12. Monday through Friday; 45 minutes; live/tape/film; 2 cameras; 1½ hours preparation. Sponsored.

Tucson, Arizona

ZIPO THE CLOWN. A busy program performed under the big top before live audience. Magic tricks, puppet skits, drawing instructions, contests (pie eating and others), are usually on agenda. Representatives of civic and charitable groups are interviewed, promote their activities. Age: preschool to 9. Saturdays; 30 minutes; live/tape/film; 2 cameras; 2 hours rehearsal; 5 hours writing and preparation. Sponsored.

Tulsa, Oklahoma

BIG BILL SHOW. Puppetry, interviews with children and special guests, child talent, art contests, and cartoons. Age: 6 to 12. Monday through Friday; 30 minutes; live/film; 3½ hours writing and preparation. Sponsored.

LEE AND LIONEL. King Lionel (a puppet) lives in a castle surrounded by a moat; an alligator scientist, a banjo-playing Koala bear, are among the inhabitants of his kingdom. Live portions of this program describe life in the castle; in addition, they bring child guests before camera in games, interviews, and demonstrations. Cartoons are shown. Representatives of Boy and Girl Scouts, hospitals, religious groups, and other organizations are frequently associated with program. Age: preschool to 12. Monday through Friday; 45 minutes; live/tape/film; 2 cameras; 30 minutes rehearsal; 8 hours preparation. Sponsored.

Valley City, North Dakota

CAPTAIN JIM. Aboard the *Sink Knot,* the host interviews young guests, lets them ring the ship's bell and fish from the dock for prizes, gives tips on safety and manners, teaches drawing, and conducts contests for viewers. Cartoons are shown at intervals. Program draws liberally from local organizations. Age: preschool to 9. Monday through Friday; 1¼ hours; live/film; 2 cameras; 30 minutes rehearsal; 2 hours preparation. Sponsored.

Washington, D.C.

PLAY SCHOOL 9. A cartoon program for preschool children with one taped educational short film offered each time. Educational shorts are written and produced by committee of area elementary educators. They cover such subjects as "Keep toys in a special place," "Friends who help us," "A visit to the dentist," " 'On' and 'under,' " "How to lace a shoe." Age: Preschool. Monday through Friday; 40 minutes; tape/film; 2 cameras; 1 hour rehearsal; 4 hours writing and preparation (for the educational short). Sponsored.

West Palm Beach, Florida

PARTY TIMERS. A program of audience participation. Children exhibit their talent, join in games and quizzes, perform experiments, listen to stories. SPCA, which is associated with production, brings animals to program, discusses their care, and so on. Age: 6 to 9. Monday through Friday; 30 minutes; live/film; 2 cameras; 4 hours preparation.

Wichita, Kansas

COWBOY FRANK AND HIS ANIMAL FRIENDS. In this animal variety program, the host and two assistants show how to feed, care for, and train animals, demonstrate animal acts, and interview zoo directors. Children bring their pets to the program. Host uses homespun philosophy to inculcate respect for parents and kindness to animals. Cartoons and birthday party are included in each program. Age: preschool to 12. Monday through Friday; 45 minutes; live/tape/film; 2 cameras; 1 hour preparation. Sponsored.

York, Pennsylvania

A VISIT WITH SANTA CLAUS. During the five weeks before Christmas, children talked to Santa on the program and Santa read cards and letters sent in by viewers. Setting was Santa's house at the North Pole with tree, gifts, and Santa's bag. Age: preschool to 9. One month only. Monday through Friday; 15 minutes; live; 2 cameras. Sponsored.

The World
of the Young Viewer

**Some Observations and Guidelines for Broadcasters
Based on Principles of Child Development**

Television programs — like all forms of communication addressed to children — are most effective when they reflect some aspect of the child's world. The adult programmer faces the problem of trying to see children's needs and desires through his — adult — eyes. But like the early writers of children's books, many American film makers and television producers have had little background in designing their product for children. In contrast, films for children have been made successfully for years in other countries, notably in England.

In this country, however, there has thus far been little occasion to integrate the findings of child development and child psychology into the creation of either films or television programs. The discussion which follows is a consideration of some principles from these fields. It includes (part I) a summary of some aspects of how the child views his world. How that world looks to the preschooler, to the child from six to nine and from nine to twelve, and to the adolescent, is described in part II. Some practical applications of the principles of child development in terms of programs and production are discussed in part III.

*Know you what it is to be a child? It is to be something
very different from man of today...It is to believe in
loveliness, to believe in belief; it is to be so little that the
elves can reach to whisper in your ear; it is to turn
pumpkins into coaches, and mice into horses, lowness
into loftiness, and nothing into everything...*

Francis Thompson, *Shelley*

I HOW THE CHILD VIEWS THE WORLD

Francis Thompson's statement is a poetic reminder that children are
not little adults and that the child's view of the world differs radically
from the adult's in a number of striking ways. Several of these differences underscore the very special world of the child and bear directly on
television program content.

The adult understands the relationship that words have to things,
but the child is still developing this ability throughout childhood. The
adult has a large fund of remembrances that provide points of reference
for his thinking, whereas the child draws on only a limited reservoir of
remembrances. The child's memory is thus not only relatively meager
but also spotty. The adult, because of his ability to think integratively,
can understand relationships that elude the child. Another difference
between adults and children is that children may be confused by the
violation of kinds of cause and effect with which they are familiar. Thus,
if an animal in a cartoon hits another animal on the head with great force
but without visible effect, the child viewer may be puzzled. A human
talking to a horse is easy to accept because it may happen, but live horses
talking to each other might be confusing because this situation would
too closely contradict the child's knowledge of the world.

Adults are likely to be bored by something that is repetitive, but
the child enjoys repetition. A child may fill up and empty a sand pail
twenty-five times and enjoy it more each time. Repetition reinforces what

the child knows. He derives very real pleasure from encountering something recognizable by its repetition and likes to stay with it.

Adults and children differ greatly in their awareness of reality and fantasy. Since the young child does not have the ability to understand symbolic meanings, presentation rather than the representation of one thing by another is necessary. Especially for the young child, a daydream is something that happens to him on a level that is just as real as his walking across the street. The adult, of course, knows the difference between daydream and reality, but for the young viewer the boundary between reality and fantasy is less distinct. What the programmer intends to be reality may be perceived by the young viewer as fantasy, and vice versa. Even a program that has a considerable fantasy content will become a part of the child's reality system if it is watched regularly over a long period of time.

One of the most significant ways in which adults and children differ in what they perceive is in the adult's ability to see perceptual wholes. The adult can see that the parts of a program contribute to a whole and that the program has a beginning, a middle, and an end. The child does not understand this, although he does anticipate that change will be part of a story or program. The child tends to view events as being distinct and unconnected, so that the events leading up to the end of a story or program are at least as important as its resolution. Since children are not fully capable of logical thought, they find it hard to believe a happy ending that obliterates the steps leading to that ending. All the parts of a program have relatively separate meanings to the young child, who will recall the episode of the wolf eating the grandmother in *Little Red Riding Hood* as easily as he recalls the happy ending.

The child's interest in the wolf eating the grandmother reminds us that behavior which adults regard as questionable is at the core of much that appeals to children. In one of the best-known children's stories, Peter Rabbit goes into a garden that his mother has warned him not to approach. Mr. McGregor threatens to cook and eat Peter, a suggestion that is rather uncivilized from an adult point of view; yet three- and four-year-olds frequently mention such cannibalistic acts! The young child is unaware of society's attitudes on this subject, and is responding to a fantasy that does not derive from the larger social system, so that the restrictions of the system have little effect on him. Content of this kind is enjoyed by a child, as he realizes that he is not alone in experiencing feelings that are alien to the adult world.

One of the boundaries that sets off the child's world from that of the adult is children's lore. Like folk tales and fables, children's lore — though not written down — is much the same from one culture and time to another. It reappears in every generation of children without any visible means of transmission. It seems to spring from children themselves; it is not learned from adults, nor is it superimposed by adult instruction. It includes tongue twisters, tales that don't end, and holiday lore. It also includes tangle talk, punning, rhyming, and catch riddles. Other aspects of children's lore are nonsense and satirical verse and calendar lore.

A second important difference is seen in children's responses to certain kinds of auditory appeals. Some are so broadly based that they almost cut across children's age, sex, and even nationality lines. The rhythm, form, word choice, and flow of poetry have deep meaning for the child. Recitation is not the only format for poetry. Music, drama, film, rhythms, and other activities, may be related to poetry. Many of the prose favorites of younger children are almost poetic in form (the Dr. Seuss books). Children like the sounds of poetry for the same reason that they enjoy making up words, as in a poem like *Eletelephony,* which is based on made-up words ("elephone"). At about the age of six there is almost a mania for rhyming, and this interest is sustained and reaches its peak between eight and ten.

Another auditory appeal that the child finds difficult to resist is provided by music. Music is almost a universal language for children because it elicits spontaneous bodily movements. Its rhythm encourages clapping, whistling, and humming. Music stimulates individualized associations and its enjoyment is not necessarily dependent on any knowledge of words and language. The young child easily learns things set to music: Some children can only recall the alphabet as they sing it to the melody of "Twinkle, Twinkle, Little Star." Young children enjoy music in syncopated or jazz arrangements. Older children may respond to narrative and descriptive music ("Peter and the Wolf," "Carnival of the Animals"), while children of all ages are fascinated by musical instruments and enjoy their exposition ("Tubby the Tuba"). The inherent movement of ballet music makes it especially useful in many contexts involving children.

Their comparative lack of understanding of the meanings of words leads children to have a unique and direct relationship to nonverbal communication. The child's fantasy activity is encouraged by program material on a nonverbal level. The younger the child, the truer this is likely to be. The appeal of the nonverbal is one reason for the extreme popularity of pantomime with children of all ages. The youngest child as well as his older brother may enjoy the relatively gross gestures of the clown. As he grows older and attempts to emulate a mime, he realizes that mimicry is a skill and develops respect for the performer.

Children enjoy clowns because they do things that the child is not permitted to do: the clown may blunder and fumble while the child must not. The child also gets a feeling of superiority by understanding the meaning of the mime's nonverbal communication: children are constantly acting things out without words. Even the older child retains an interest in gestures and actions as a fond remnant of his earlier interest. The peak of interest in pantomime is between nine and twelve.

It is all too easy for the adult to assume that verbal communication is easy for the child. "Abracadabra" is a signal to many adults that something magical will happen, but a child generally does not require such a word if he sees a magician holding a wand that is about to move. This is one reason for the enormous popularity of film and television cartoons, which are semiabstract and depend on movement, activity, and sound effects rather than actual words. The semiabstractness of cartoons makes it easy for children to take in a complete scene, and their use of basic shapes and forms conveys a visual sense of repetition. Their simplified forms make it easy to focus attention when compared with the complexities of observing real-life scenes. Cartoons rely so heavily on motion that it becomes possible for even the very young child to observe the movement. On the basis of the observed movement, he can note changes in a scene and begin to apply his reasoning capacity.

There are certain recurrent themes in children's fiction which are so popular that they have become classics. Although an adult classic is often something that adults shun, a children's classic is likely to have enormous and continuing appeal for children because its content is so meaningful to them. The child who loses his parent and is reunited with him *(Curious George)*, the weak brother who is ultimately stronger than his brothers *(Hop o' My Thumb)*, the parentless child who triumphs over villainy *(Treasure Island)*, and the double-image twin *(The Prince and the Pauper)* are examples of universal themes that strike a responsive chord in children of all ages. Classics like these are so popular that they also appear on over thirty different record labels.

We do not know the details of how television affects children's values. We do know that children typically absorb values from their families and the other persons with whom they are in regular contact and to whom they are significantly attached. A child is therefore likely to derive values from television to the extent that such values are congruent with his underlying personality as this has derived from persons and groups that are meaningful to him. As the naturalist John Muir said, "You can see a bird in a bush only if you have one in your heart." If, on the other hand, the child has no relevant values stemming either from personality or from social background, television may help to provide them.

Identification with the people on the television screen is difficult for a young child. Although he is very dependent on others, the young child cannot think in terms of others or put himself in another's place. Whether or not he can completely identify with the people on the screen, the child will be able to relate to them only to the extent that he has prior experience with such people. Thus, the orbital flights of the Soviet space travelers—reported entirely after the fact—were relatively unreal and meaningless to American children, who could not even remember the cosmonauts' names. When, however, television enabled the children to watch and *participate* in the flights and their preparation by the United States astronauts, the children were able to begin relating to the events and the men of Project Mercury.

II THE DEVELOPING CHILD AND HIS DEVELOPING INTERESTS

A continuing problem for the broadcaster is to determine what program content is appropriate for children at different ages. Child development offers clues that may help in making this determination. The child's viewing will be an active process to the extent that the program content is complementary to his needs. A young viewer can relate only to what his development has made it possible for him to understand. A youngster of four cannot relate to a current social problem.

One difficulty in the way of matching age levels with program types is that the further we move away from infancy, the less exact is any cataloging of interests by age. Another difficulty is that there is some overlap. While children are likely to regard as "kid stuff" material that has been of interest to them in the past, they will tend to be interested in programs directed to the next higher age level as well as to their own.

It is important to note that the generalizations that can be made about child development apply to both boys and girls, and no real need exists to create separate programs for each sex, even if this were practical. One way of regarding the different age levels in the child viewing population is to classify them into the preschooler, who is under the age of six; the six-to-nine, who is in the lower grades at elementary school and is on the juvenile level; the nine-to-twelve or preadolescent; and the adolescent, who is thirteen or more.

The child is his own reference point in his earliest years, and then gradually grows and matures. His evolution from being completely self-centered is brought about by his trying to find his proper role in his family, among his peers, and in society. The evolving patterns stemming from the child's needs are reflected in the activities and interests that characterize each major age level.

THE PRESCHOOLER: CENTER OF HIS UNIVERSE

It is possible to make some valid generalizations about the preschooler, even though there are enormous differences within this level. The child of four is likely to be defiant of his parents, but at five he is a "little angel" and is almost "too good." By six, he is demanding and vigorous again.

Preschoolers see things in a very personal way. They are likely to attribute qualities of life to inanimate objects. They may think that clouds move under their own power. Some few children even believe that the characters on a television screen are little people who live and sleep in the set behind the screen!

Time does not exist as a concept for the preschooler. There is little awareness of time that is past. "Once upon a time" or "a long, long time ago" have as much—or as little—meaning for him as "before you were born." The preschooler is likely to be aware of yesterday or last Christmas, his last birthday, and similar personally toned dates, but not of more general concepts of the past. Time in the future is even less understandable. One reason for the young child's difficulties with time is that it is so closely related to numbers, which are relatively complicated concepts and which he normally only begins to understand and apply at school.

Fairy tales, especially those of Grimm, represent material that is of extraordinary importance to the young child because it fulfills so many of his needs. Fairy tales have a small number of characters, and the adult characters are like children. Action is concentrated and simple. There are fabulous beings—dwarfs, giants, and dragons. All of the characters are essentially types. The animals in fairy tales do interesting things. Some eventually become people, like the Frog Prince, so that the talking of animals in fairy tales does not seem strange to children. By the age of four, a child is able to follow the plot of a fairy tale.

Perhaps his small size in a world of large people with great power over him makes it especially easy for the preschooler to enjoy a story in which the youngest or smallest or shyest member of a group achieves a high goal, as in the tale of the ugly duckling who becomes a beautiful swan. Children of this age often have fantasies about being big. Perhaps this is one reason for the success of *Cinderella*. The youngest and smallest child, Cinderella grows up rapidly and gets married—and to a prince!

Many fairy tales *(Jack and the Beanstalk,* for example), have a conflict between a young person and an older person, often of the same sex. The younger person almost always triumphs over the older and stronger one. The tales are often concerned with relationships between a child and benign and powerful persons of the opposite sex. They vividly contrast good and bad. The adult characters often have great power. These characteristics of fairy tales are similar to important aspects of the life of the preschool child.

Fairy tales may provide a catharsis for feelings, a happy resolution of a relevant conflict situation, and a constructive taste for mastery of the conflict. While every attempt must be made to avoid the saccharine in presenting them, the vigor of many fairy tales requires an emphasis on the fabulous and wonderful. A prince who is a typically handsome young American man will be puzzling to the child viewer. The young child's difficulties in distinguishing between fabulation and truth help to make the fairy tale of even greater interest to him. They also demand that the presentation clearly avoid the realistic.

Because of his great preoccupation with himself, the preschooler is likely to respond to television to the extent that he has the feeling that people on the screen represent an audience for him. Programs that provide the opportunity to talk, to sing, to clap, and to imitate in response to what is happening on the screen offer children psychologically healthy avenues of expression. Programs that permit the child to respond in this way with a minimum of equipment are likely to be successful with the preschooler. "Simon Says," rhythms, and singing are examples of such activities. Instruments like clappers or tambourines are desirable because of the interest of young people in repetitive patterns. Nursery songs dealing with a wide variety of matters, including relatively "serious" topics like safety, health, and science, are also of interest to the preschooler if they are repetitive and rhythmical.

THE SIX- TO NINE-YEAR-OLD: WIDENING HORIZONS

It is even more difficult to generalize about the middle-level child than about the preschooler, since he seems to change from year to year. Thus, a seven-year-old is typically morose and likes to be alone. The eight-year-old generally is expansive and enjoys meeting the world. Although at nine he is likely to be rebellious and independent, at ten the child is likely to be satisfied with life and with himself.

The juvenile of six to nine is likely to be making his first significant contacts with the world beyond the family. He dilutes the intensity of the immediate family environment by expanding his interest to school and friends. He is relatively malleable and interested in sharing with his peers. As he approaches nine he becomes interested in competitive sports that involve teamwork and mutual goals, like baseball. He is developing a growing need to associate with other young people of his age and is less content with the world of authoritarian adults who have been taking care of him. He may express this need to look outward by an interest in wars and submarines and in pilots and other adventurers.

The child begins to become fascinated by pirates, Indians, and characters like Robinson Crusoe and Tom Sawyer. In such stories, good and bad are presented in stereotype, and children are generally portrayed as being dignified and important. The boys and girls in such fiction are more active and have more distinct personalities than do children in fairy tales. The stories of interest to children in this age group are often concerned with the attempts of the characters, while in the company of their friends, to acquire knowledge and social skill. They often overcome considerable obstacles. Ongoing social situations involving people like those in the *Bobbsey Twins, Nancy Drew,* or *The Hardy Boys* series are of great interest. Adults in the stories are generally introduced incidentally and are benign. They get along well with the child characters. These characteristics of the fiction popular with the juvenile level are in line with the emotional requirements of children at this age.

NINE TO TWELVE: THE UNIVERSE EXPANDS

Beginning at around the age of nine and continuing to approximately twelve, there occurs the "quiet miracle of preadolescence." The preadolescent is interested in values and responds to fairly sophisticated expressions of morality. One of these expressions is represented by Bible stories, which appeal to children of nine or more. The complicated nature of many Bible stories and their occasional violence make it necessary to select them carefully. Holidays or festivals are appropriate occasions for stories from the Bible or other religious sources.

School children of this age are studying foreign countries and picaresque aspects of their country's past. They show a keen interest in unusual settings. This may be one reason for the great interest in ghost, mystery, and detective stories that begins around age nine. During this period, children show involvement with biography, which seems to be of special interest to girl viewers, with their traditional interest in people. Both boys and girls, however, respond to biographies. They not only bring the youngster close to the world of a famous person, but also give him the impression that he is hobnobbing with the mighty by mentioning relatively trivial incidents.

Biographies may be fanciful, and some children's classics even have historical figures chatting with animals *(Mr. Revere and I, I Discover Columbus, Ben and Me)*. Biographies, like stories dealing with the past, give the child experience in deriving pleasure from things that have already happened and may lead him to get more pleasure from his own frequently hazy memories. The fantasy of the past may thus actually help to improve the child's contact with his own understanding of reality.

Preadolescence appears to be the ideal age for introducing the epics. Once the child has gone to school and been exposed to a succession of teachers, he has begun to think of heroes other than his parents. The child is also interested in folklore and epics because gods and men in these sagas are in competition with one another, and competition is becoming increasingly important to the child. Because the epics and sagas deal with fabulous half-man, half-god characters who are so far removed in time and place, the child's anxiety in following their activities is minimal. The epic heroes personify themes of almost universal interest to children in this age group. For the same reason, characters like Paul Bunyan appeal to them.

THE ADOLESCENT: SEARCH FOR SELF

By thirteen, the child is an adolescent. His interest in the opposite sex is translated into a concern about matters of reality in his reading and television viewing. Perhaps reflecting the conflict that characterizes adolescence, he enjoys fiction that is about realistic persons in situations of conflict *(Life on the Mississippi;* the works of O. Henry and Bret Harte). Poetry that is concerned with conflict *(The Highwayman;* the poems of Heine and Shakespeare) is also very appealing. The built-in conflict of sports makes this period the peak of interest in competitive sports activities. The challenge posed by nature and by science gives these two subjects a special niche for the teenager.

It is a rare teenager who has not, however fleetingly, thought of the possibility of becoming an actor. This recurrent fantasy, combined with the intrinsic conflict of drama, makes drama a preferred format for this age group. The teenager's interest in biography is a reflection of his preoccupation with the social in all of its meanings. One facet of this is his growing awareness of foreign countries and of news and current events and their personalities. Another is his great interest in clothing.

The interest in hobbies that characterized the earlier years has changed. Some youngsters have become committed hobbyists while others have abandoned their former interest. The teenager's concern with the contemporary scene is so great that his interest in nonfiction reaches what is probably its developmental maximum as his interest in fairy tales and similar material wanes. Although the peak of outgoingness comes at eleven, by thirteen and adolescence the child has begun turning back to a more self-centered viewpoint. The adolescent's preoccupation with himself differs from that of the preschooler. The younger child is isolated because he has little awareness of others and their roles. The adolescent is concerned with himself because he is so aware of others that he has misgivings about how he will affect them.

*   *   *

As we observe the child in the years from preschool to adolescence, we note the parallels between his own growth and developmental profile and the patterns of his growing and expanding interests. The child who, at two, clutched his parent's hand tight as they crossed the street may, at thirteen, be picking up Istanbul on a "ham" radio. By stages, his world has grown. Through it all, however, certain interest areas common to all age levels have persisted while the child's approach to them has become more sophisticated. The broadcaster interested in children's programming can adapt much available material in ways that will be appealing at each of the children's age levels.

Humor   Humor appeals to all children. Laughter is one way in which children can cope with difficulties and feel powerful. It helps to relieve tension in many different kinds of programs, just as it does when a child interjects humor as one way of coping with a reality situation. A joke, a silly gesture, or a riddle represent ways of easing tension that a child appreciates. The preschooler enjoys jokes based on names and name reversals. He understands physical humor and silliness. The child of six to nine enjoys silliness, especially when it blends into nonsense in verbalisms, as in the works of Edward Lear and Lewis Carroll. He begins at this time to think in terms of verbal jokes. The favorite joke in this age group is likely to be the joking riddle, which often deals with some-one who is not bright and does things that the child would not do. Some kinds of humorous content, as in the *Just-So Stories,* appeal to both the juvenile and the preadolescent. The nine-to-twelve youngster is fairly sophisticated, enjoys double meanings and parody, and is beginning to understand satire (Gilbert and Sullivan). The child of thirteen or more begins to enjoy the shaggy dog story.

Holidays   There are many holiday situations that have a related but slightly different appeal for each age group and that lend themselves to programming. For example, the Hallowe'en holiday gives the young-ster under six a chance to sing, to make masks, and to enjoy lighting candles. The juvenile enjoys making masks, hearing short stories about the holiday, and watching games like bobbing for apples. The nine-to-twelve child is ready for holiday ghost and mystery stories that may be acted out. The child of thirteen or more is interested in the macabre aspects of the holiday and in poetry about it.

Physical Exercises   Exercise also offers something for each age group, and is probably the easiest step-by-step activity in which children can engage. It appeals to practically all children. The preschooler enjoys its rhythmic qualities and its use of imitation. The juvenile likes not only the imitative aspects, but the skill it requires. The preadolescent enjoys the physical-fitness and variety aspects of exercise because of his growing interest in his body. He enjoys comparing himself with others doing the same exercises. The adolescent, acutely aware of his body, seeks out procedures, like exercise, that help him to develop it.

Drawing and Painting   The art lesson is another popular television activity that provides a wide range of response among different age groups. The preschooler will be scribbling, mostly as a muscular control device, and vertical strokes will precede the horizontal. His arm will swing in arclike movements. He is likely to use a number of symbols. The six- to nine-year-old enjoys experimenting and variation. Although he can make a picture of almost anything, he has usually developed a number of favorite subjects. His work is likely to have considerable disproportion, and certain motifs like war and farm life are common. The preadolescent is likely to be painting subjects based on television program material. Boys will be doing vehicles and rockets; girls will paint animals, especially horses. In these years just before puberty there is a low level of aesthetic interest, and the personal-expression element is minimal. The child of thirteen or more reestablishes an interest in self-expression and art appreciation.

Magic   Perhaps because it reflects the child's earlier feelings of omnipotence, magic on television interests the young viewer at every age level. Relatively visible tricks like pulling a rabbit out of a hat or pulling a bouquet out of a thin wand are best because of their startling visual incongruity. The child under six enjoys magic because of its incongruity, while the youngster of six to nine likes to look at magic, but doesn't know how it is done or why it is a trick. By the time the preadolescent observes the trick, he gets a feeling of superiority from determining how it is worked. He watches, for example, for the moment when the paper flowers open up in the bouquet trick. The adolescent may be learning to do the trick. Not only the formal magic, but the character who is a wonder worker and who effects magic is very popular with the preschool as well as the six-to-nine group. Such children's classics as *Dr. Dolittle, Mary*

Poppins, and *The Wind in the Willows* share this quality. The wonder worker's age or appearance, which may be strange, is less important than his ability to engage in magic. From interest in magic animals (as in *Winnie-the-Pooh*) as a preschooler, the child progresses to an interest in magic objects in the six-to-nine group. For example, the magic cap (worn by the witch in *The Wizard of Oz),* the magic cloak (Caliph Haroun al-Rashid), or magic boots *(Puss in Boots)* are disguises that permit their wearers to do strange and wonderful things. The nine- to twelve-year-old moves a step closer to reality with heroes who have magic shields (Jason), magic girdles (Minerva), magic sandals (Mercury), or a symbolically magical slingshot (David). For the children in this age group, the objects associated with these characters are symbolic identifications rather than disguises. The adolescent's interest in magic involves science fiction and romanticizing aspects of the past.

Nature and Animals   Nature situations are of interest to different age groups. The preschooler enjoys a variety of situations involving animal characters, whose few but significant features make it easy for the child to project himself to the animal. Pets give a child a feeling of the regularity of nature. Seeing the growth of a living thing that is small is very reassuring to the child and helps him to feel big. The pet is a companion who helps to replace the "imaginary playmate" of the preschooler and helps him to prepare for meeting the real playmates he will have at school. Inasmuch as children have to be taught how to play together, even with a pet, a pet program is a good vehicle for such learning.

The six- to nine-year-old child enjoys animal stories that are obviously close representations of human situations. Thus *Bambi,* which deals with a doe and her young, gives a clear picture of the human mother-child relationship. The child of nine to twelve is more concerned with the world outside the home and is likely to enjoy stories of relationships between animals and children like *Lassie.* Such material includes many stories with young heroines and thus program content of special interest to girls. It also provides an acceptable outlet for showing tenderness, which today is as difficult to express on television as elsewhere. By adolescence, the child's earlier symbolic interest in animals is replaced by a more realistic view of animals and their relationship to human beings. Another desirable aspect of programs involving animals is that animals do things that the child likes but is rarely permitted to do, like playing with water and mud. The viewer can obtain a secondary gratification by seeing animals engaging in those activities. The child who modifies his own needs in accordance with the realistic demands of society can express related needs through enjoying such program content.

Fables Animals figure prominently among the nonhuman characters in fables, which represent a format that is very important to children. Fables are ideal television fare because they are generally in dialogue form and have a small cast of characters. The simple plot of the very short story leads directly to a climax. It can be adapted for acting by puppets or children. The child enjoys fables because the maxim that caps the moral is usually something that the child has heard from adults. The maxim, like the proverb that it resembles, enables the child vicariously to visit the adult world. The universal themes of fables appear in many different cultures. The preschooler enjoys the nonhuman characters *(The Hare and the Tortoise)*, while the juvenile likes the plot interplay *(The Wind and the Sun)*. The preadolescent is enthusiastic about the moral *(The Fox and the Grapes)*. The adolescent's interest in fables has turned into an interest in allegory *(Everyman)*.

Fantasy The extraordinarily powerful adults who do so much to whet the interest of the preschooler in Grimm's fairy tales are likely to be replaced by less powerful adults in Andersen's fairy tales. Andersen's themes and his delicacy of style *(The Little Match Girl)* appeal to the child of six to nine. The more complicated imagery and literary qualities of the fairy tales of Andrew Lang hold the attraction of the juvenile and even of many adolescents. By nine, the preadolescent is also likely to begin enjoying the fairy tales of Oscar Wilde, with their poignant and sensitive moralistic qualities. He is also likely to enjoy fairy tales from other countries, especially those from the Orient, Ireland ("little people"), and Russia. Such stories come from countries and cultures far enough from our own to be new, and yet, because of their content, are not excessively strange. For example, he enjoys observing how the theme of the swan is handled in foreign fairy tales, while painlessly learning a great deal about cultures that have used this theme.

Preadolescents enjoy fairy tales not only for their themes but because they enjoy looking for the incidental clues which will be used in the resolution of the story. Children get a feeling of mastery as they figure out what will happen on the basis of clues scattered throughout the story. One reason children in this age group stay with a fairy tale is to see if it will end the way that the clues suggest it will end. The preadolescent is likely to be enjoying many stories based on fancy that are very similar to fairy tales, although they are more sophisticated. Thus, *The Borrowers* and *The Hobbit* are about little people who have a separate society. *Stuart Little, The Great Geppy,* and *The Three Policemen* are other examples of stories in this category that are extremely popular with youngsters in this age group. The previous interest of the youngster in fairy tales leads in a logical progression to the preadolescent's great enthusiasm for myths, legends, folklore, and other fantasy material. Perhaps because the preadolescent is relatively less receptive to the new and different than when he was younger, he accepts this material as a continuation of his earlier interest in fairy tales. The adolescent is interested in fabulous people who are nonetheless real, like Theodore Roosevelt, Madame Curie, or Einstein.

III SOME PRACTICAL APPLICATIONS

In addition to suggesting program material to the broadcaster, some of the findings in the study of child development have relevance to practical problems of programming and production. In this chapter an effort is made, in terms of specifics, to indicate how these principles may be applied. They range from language to personalities, from photography to pretesting.

Language It is important for the programmer to realize the special qualities of the child's language. Formal definitions are relatively difficult even for a child of nine. The grammatical structure used with the preschooler and the six-to-nine-year-old is best kept very simple. Nouns, pronouns, and verbs are the most important parts of sentences, which should be as brief and explicit as possible. Adverbs and adjectives can be minimized. The growing vocabulary and ability to comprehend more complex sentence structure of the nine-to-twelve group gives the writer for such children much greater freedom. The child of thirteen is able to understand most of the standard adult vocabulary and is especially aware of current idiom.

New material is best presented in terms of the familiar in accordance with the ability of different age groups to comprehend different kinds of content. The preschooler cannot discern differences in verbal contexts, although he may discern visual or auditory differences. As the child becomes older he becomes aware of physical differences and is then able to begin to understand differences implied in language. When shown a dime and a penny, a three-year-old notes only that they seem to be of different colors. A five-year-old would probably know that the dime is smaller but is worth more, although he could not express this difference in words. He would, however, be able to understand, in *Goldilocks and the Three Bears,* the differences between the biggest bowl of porridge, which the father bear had, and the smallest bowl, which the baby bear had. The seven-year-old would know that he could buy more with the dime, even though it was smaller. By the age of nine or so, he could verbalize the essential difference between the coins in terms of purchasing power.

In trying to make a comparison understandable to the nine-to-twelve-year-old group, we might, for example, use a single stick figure as a pictograph to represent the population of the United States in 1790. A number of larger stick figures could represent the population today. Even with the child of thirteen or more, it is useful to make comparisons as frequently as possible. Thus, to say that England has a certain population living on a certain number of square miles is less effective than to say that the country of England is a little smaller than the state of Oregon but has almost thirty-four times as many people living in it.

Names of Characters The names given to characters in children's television programs may be extremely important, because of the close relationship between the performer and the name in the child's mind. Many children's programs feature characters with extremely bizarre names that do not contribute to the movement or progress of the program. A number of names of characters on children's programs represent humor on an adult's rather than a child's level (e.g., Billy Baldpate). Children enjoy a funny name, but only if it is funny to them. In general, children are likely to enjoy relatively short names that provide a chance to mouth enjoyable sounds (e.g., Hoja). Children enjoy mouthing sounds because of the sheer physical pleasure it provides, almost independently of the sounds' meaning.

Voices Every voice in a children's television program ought to have a visible origin because of the ease with which children may be frightened by a voice that seems to have no source. One reason an eerie laugh is frightening to many young viewers is that its origin is usually obscure. Voices that are too shrill, except in the cast of nonhuman characters or puppets, are likely to disturb the child, and unusually deep voices may be frightening. Ventriloquists' dummies that look lifelike may also be frightening. Often their voices sound human, and it is very difficult for the child to understand just what these creatures are. An adult who pretends to talk in a child's voice will be unbelievable because the child may compare the adult's voice with the voices of adults he has known and note the incongruity.

Staging   Staging in children's programs is even more important than it is in programs for adults because a number of the established technical procedures of television must be modified for the child audience.

The traditional long shot—medium shot—medium close-up sequence is well suited to give the young viewer a growing feeling of involvement with what is happening. This sequence is one way of assisting children to assimilate the action. However, because the child does not ordinarily have a field of vision comparable to the extreme close-up, care must first be taken to orient the viewer to the object in relation to its environment. In presenting educational material, this is done by "dollying in" on the specimen to be viewed. Overuse of close-ups prevents the child from selecting specific background or foreground aspects of a scene, and many young children have a greater need to look and select rather than to see. For obvious reasons, faces that fill the screen should be avoided. A long fade-out is also likely to be confusing, because the young viewer is so much more involved in action that happens quickly. A long fade-out has connotations of space and time that may be difficult for the child to understand. Similarly, abrupt shifts of scene or sequence can be confusing.

Clear camera work and lighting are likely to be appreciated by children, who tend to follow action in pictures rather than through dialogue. The child responds to movement on the screen because of his own strong interest in movement. He is therefore likely to enjoy a program more if it has considerable movement. If there are sections of a program in which none of the characters speaks, the child may be able to respond to the people on the screen by talking with or about them.

Program Structure   Ideally, a program starts its action promptly and presents the important characters fairly early. A character who does not have a clear-cut function is likely to be confusing. If there is a climax, it ideally occurs just before the end of the program.

The serial format not only maintains interest, but often lends itself to appropriate subclimaxes. The young viewer enjoys serials because of his anticipation of the next episode. This is especially true of the child of eight or more who has the ability to foresee and anticipate events. Children enjoy serials so much that even lengthy material may lend itself to serialization, as did Dickens's novels. There are many children's classics (*Gulliver's Travels, Alice in Wonderland,* the James Willard Schultz westerns) that are especially appropriate for serialization.

A musical signature that is used to introduce a program is one way of establishing its mood and of helping young viewers to feel their way into the program. Many boys and girls are extremely alert to background music, which can be just as suggestive as plot, characters, action, and setting and which deserves much attention.

The different age groups respond to different program elements and formats. For the preschooler, play and observation are basic attention-holding devices. An anthology or variety format would be appropriate for the child of six to twelve, who can relate to different kinds of activities fairly easily. The adolescent can enjoy a wide variety of content without feeling a need to compare one thing with another. The preschooler, in contrast, would not be able to enjoy too many different kinds of things.

The different age groups have different kinds of attention levels. The preschooler finds the small details on the screen more interesting than its major content and focuses on the details. The juvenile tends to overlook details and to see wholes, while paying little attention to background. The child of nine to twelve sees both foreground and background, takes in the scene, and looks for clues in both scenery and action to the sequences that are to follow. The thirteen-year-old responds to specific personalities and is on his way to becoming an active fan of the personalities.

The Program Host   Hosts ought to be minimally authoritarian, especially on programs for the preschooler. Otherwise they may remind the youngster of authoritarian adults who may have been sources of disappointment. How the host walks and sits, his gestures and other nonverbal communication, may be more important to the child viewer than what he says. A hostess who looks and sounds like a schoolmarm stereotype of a teacher is likely to be unfavorably received by young people.

One useful image of the host is a kind of good aunt or good uncle with whom the child likes to do things. Such a nonauthority figure is not threatening and cannot affect the child's daily reward and punishment system, even by implication. A host who is pleasantly and quietly dressed is likely to have rapport with large groups in the child audience. A host of forty who is pretending to be ten and dresses accordingly is likely to strain the credulity of even the youngest viewer.

Other Adult Roles   The selection of adults other than the host to appear on children's programs is important. Parents are probably best presented as relatively young because the young child's sense of time leads him to see his own parents as young. It is important to remember that the principal character or hero to a child viewer may not be the person officially playing the role of hero; he may be a minor character, the antagonist, or another "heavy." Therefore, considerable care must go into selecting even secondary characters.

Child Performers   The young viewer is likely to have a rather complex relationship to young children who are shown on camera. He feels that he belongs to the group on the screen, so that child performers should ideally look and behave like real children rather than professional actors; a really polished child performer will arouse rancor in the young viewer. (In the same way, Deanna Durbin and Shirley Temple, because they were so extremely talented and charming, irritated many young moviegoers in the 1930s.)

Inasmuch as the child projects himself into the activity on the television screen, it is probable that a minimum of children on camera is desirable. The child can thus see himself with the host and with others in the program and have less resentment of the children who are actually shown. The greater opportunity the child viewer has to project himself into the group on the screen, the happier he is likely to be. (Some of the success of Arthur Godfrey's television program derived from the reaction of the typical woman viewer who saw herself as Mrs. Godfrey because no performer corresponding to Mrs. Godfrey was shown.)

Another hazard of having children on camera, in addition to the difficulties of controlling what they will say, is that there is an almost unavoidable tendency for the performer or host to begin "playing" to them rather than to the audience at home.

In putting a child in front of a television camera, the director is essentially presenting the viewer to himself. For this reason, a preschooler or six-to-nine-year-old youngster may respond favorably to a "bad" cat or puppet but will not respond favorably to a "bad" little boy or girl on camera. This kind of confrontation is likely to irritate young people, perhaps because it may be too close to home.

Studio Audience   The question of children in the studio audience is a recurring one. A studio audience helps a program from a promotional standpoint. However, the logistical difficulties involved in getting children into a studio to serve as an audience may be so formidable that the utility of the audience is questionable, with the possible exception of a program featuring a clown. Another reason for questioning the desirability of a studio audience is that although the child wants to feel grown-up, he may feel threatened if he gets too good an opportunity to "be" an adult. The children in the studio audience are forced to behave in a grown-up manner and thus may be resented by the viewer at home, who feels threatened by seeing these children acting this way.

Television's Special Aptitudes   Television has its own unique qualities which can be successfully used by directors. The traditional comment that the small size of the television screen contracts space and makes it difficult to present many kinds of material is perhaps less significant than the fact that the small screen may help the young viewer to feel himself its master. The small size of the screen can also stimulate the young viewer's imagination rather than confine it, if the program is staged for the eye and ear and imagination of the child. A child's program can be a "spectacular," not in the sense of a swirling and large canvas, but in the intelligent use of the kinds of things that children enjoy.

There are relatively few stories or situations that cannot be presented effectively on television—even material that is spectacular in the traditional sense. One of the outstanding examples of a motion picture of this kind was "The Thief of Baghdad" (1940). This film is often mentioned as one of the most remarkable examples of the special qualities of the film medium. Although the full sweep of a film screen is not possible on a 21-inch screen, a television version of this for children could show things that were as magical and fabulous in their way as was the movie. The genie could be shown coming out of a bottle. By using montage and appropriate background stills, he could be shown between two mountain ranges, thus suggesting his enormous size. By the deepening of his voice as he laughed and by the use of echoes, the illusion of a high voice booming through the valley could be created.

One memorable feature of this film was the number of characters who could move freely through the air. Levitation seems to be of almost universal interest to children of all ages. One of the reasons for the success of earlier mass media figures like Buck Rogers was their apparent ability to defy gravity and "fly." Because this kind of magic is so appealing to young people, program producers and technicians should be stimulated to find ways to create such effects simply and economically. Their efforts can be rewarded not only by overwhelming viewer approval, but by the consciousness of making imaginative use of some of the most exciting qualities of the television medium.

Attitudes and Anxieties Situations in which children are insolent to authority figures in the adult world (e.g., policemen) are likely to reinforce negative attitudes toward such officials. Even though a character may use bad grammar or mispronounce words or engage in name calling for humorous purposes, the child may not be able to recognize the humorous intent. For example, cartoons with Oriental characters who use the *l* sound for *r* repeat and reinforce certain stereotypes. The perpetuation of such stereotypes is contrary to current approaches in education.

Threats of violence directed toward animals with which they identify (horses, dogs) make the children themselves feel threatened. Other situations that may frighten young viewers are those in which a character with whom they identify is threatened; stories in which the identity of the "good" character is not clear; situations in which a real fear of a child, like the fear of darkness, is suggested; and those in which the viewer is too young for a particular stressful situation. Verbal aggression may be more disturbing than physical aggression, especially between parental prototypes. A threatening situation that has not yet been resolved at the conclusion of the broadcast may also be frightening to children. The more distant and unusual a character is, the more difficulty a child may have in identifying with him and the less troubled the child is likely to be by his behavior. Scenes that are capable of alarming young people are likely to be less frightening if they are shown with many characters on camera or as long shots. Either-or kinds of characters that are clear-cut, as in the westerns, are likely to be minimally disturbing. In a family-situation program, a child character may continually get into trouble without disturbing the child viewer, who knows that the character is essentially good and will be out of trouble before long. An essential consideration is whether the child views the situation as manageable or overwhelming.

PROGRAMS INVOLVING DOING

Programs for children that involve doing things are likely to be of maximum effectiveness if they *present* rather than *instruct*. Recognition of this has resulted in a wide variety of such programs. Properly applied, principles of child development can contribute to their effectiveness.

The ability to demonstrate that other children have actually made or done something is a spur toward getting child viewers interested in a task. The child feels the task is more feasible for him if a peer has completed it. One reason for difficulties in getting some children to follow through on tasks is that they may not be sympathetically involved with the host if he comes across as being almost irritatingly well informed. Another problem is that in this situation, as in most other kinds of learning, a child may drop out of completing a task at the very first step at which he encounters problems. Continuous television viewing also makes it difficult for some children to execute tasks because they are eager to watch the next program, which may deal with something quite different.

Follow-up that involves the school and the home is most useful. The young viewer's interest is likely to be enhanced by a fan club that is related to the completion of tasks presented on the program and a newsletter that outlines the matters to be taken up. To encourage the completion of tasks and continued viewing, it is helpful to involve the young viewer with the program by inviting him to send in a note about things he has made or done or problems he has met.

The ideal program does not require things that are inaccessible to the child or that may be frowned upon by his parents because they may dirty the house. For example, shadow games and shows provide an outlet for fantasy and also make it possible to tell interesting stories, with a minimum of material. The preschooler enjoys the fantasy element in these shadow games, while the child of six to nine begins to imitate some of the more difficult things shown, and the child from nine to twelve enjoys not only perfecting what is shown, but also improvising his own materials. Adolescents enjoy making silhouettes of celebrities as well as silhouette acting.

Gardening   Gardening is an example of the kind of program that requires a minimum of equipment. The preschooler can learn how things grow by carrying out simple projects like growing birdseed in a sponge, making a lima bean grow vines, or planting a sweet potato or onion that grows. The child from six to nine can plant seeds for both flowers and vegetables and become aware of different kinds of house plants and trees. From nine to twelve, he can enjoy a terrarium and learn flower arranging. Micro-photography of plant life and the activities of botanists like Luther Burbank can be fascinating to adolescents. Many of these activities would be of special appeal to the city youngster because they can be done indoors with practically no equipment. The psychological value to the child of having something grow as a result of his taking care of it is incalculable. There is not only a feeling of mastery, but also an intimacy with and understanding of nature—and pride in what is being done. Such under-standing is broadened by the child's ability to identify trees and plants. Guests, film clips, music, and trips make such a program even more interesting.

If programs of this kind step beyond the strict "how to" and offer auxiliary knowledge, they are likely to be popular. Hobby shows, which appeal to children from the age of eight upward, can easily employ such built-in content of interest to the young viewer. For example, stamp programs can discuss the people, places, events, birds, buildings, and animals shown on the stamps from various countries. Coin programs can explore the relatively unusual and mysterious aspects of coins.

Handicrafts   One kind of program that appeals to children of eight or more is concerned with knitting, embroidering, crocheting, and sewing. Children are pleased that their motor manipulatory skills are advanced enough for them to engage in such handicrafts. Girls take to this kind of program more enthusiastically than they do to "how-to" programs that are geared to either sex or to the budding scientist. This kind of handiwork program also attracts boys. For both boys and girls, making something of one's own by acquiring the requisite skills is exciting. The many adult men who have won prizes for their handiwork are popular guests on programs of this kind.

Cooking   Another program for this age group that can be undertaken with a minimum of exotic materials is a cooking program. It is hardly news to parents that boys and girls enjoy eating and that their socializing usually involves preparing and consuming food. Children are often more interested in experimenting with various kinds of food than their parents may assume. Boys can be especially interested in cooking because it is almost a treat for them to cook. Cooking represents one way of entering the adult world that is both adventuresome and of immediate use.

PUPPETRY

Puppetry on television is attractive to children both in terms of their viewing puppet programs and their being able to make and use puppets. By the age of four, a child can work a simple bag puppet; by five, he can work with puppets made of crepe paper; from six to eight, with puppets made of papier mâché, felt, and socks. From nine to twelve, the child can work with more complex puppets and with simple marionettes, while the adolescent enjoys more complex marionettes. Puppetry helps to develop human relations, develop muscular skill in a creative art form, improve speech development, and stimulate social values.

Puppets can engage in the most soaring flights of fancy and imagination. They lend themselves to magical effects, transformations, and the representation of characters who are beyond human capabilities. Because puppet activity is so concentrated, keeping puppets on screen for over forty minutes will probably tax even an enthusiastic viewer. Ten minutes is a good average length of time for a scene involving a puppet. Because of their great potential for animation, puppets are expected to be active, not motionless, when on screen.

The puppet is almost the ideal vehicle for the preschooler because the puppet can do everything the young child does—talk to itself, do interesting things, put on plays, and even have dreams. Just as the preschooler may use different voices in talking to himself or "being" different people, so is he likely to enjoy stories in which different characters are revealed by differences in their voices. A puppet is one of the few creatures who can have several voices without seeming incongruous. The preschooler can project himself into the puppet's many different roles because puppets can "understand" and "share" the child's fantasies. The juvenile from six to nine is likely to have had experience in making and using puppets and can try to improve his skill and enjoy the skill of the puppeteer. The preadolescent can enjoy the more sophisticated puppet work and use advanced puppets such as Javanese shadow puppets. A puppet show can appeal to all of these age groups simultaneously.

The repetitive and therefore predictable nature of the puppets' tricks is another major reason that children find puppets so enjoyable. Quite naturally, they identify the name of Punch from the frequency with which he punches Judy. Puppetry permits the young viewer to anticipate what will happen and to enjoy it just before it does happen as well as when it happens. Thus, a puppet clown may attempt a task twice and fail, but the viewer knows that he will succeed the third time. Both the puppet and the viewer pretend that they do not know what went wrong the first two times.

Puppets may be used in preference to child performers as actors and are less threatening than child actors might be. The unusual voices of both puppets and marionettes are likely to have a special appeal to young people. The obviously "fake" qualities of the voices may be stimulating to the child, who can enjoy imitating them. Puppets are ideal vehicles to carry fantasy material; they represent much that is comparable to the life of the young child. In presenting puppet programs, however, the broadcaster should above all avoid the cuteness with which they are so often staged.

PRETESTING

Many broadcasters are concerned about how their program will fare with children because the vast differences between adults and children mean that special criteria must be applied in the case of a child audience. Modifications of the procedures that have been found useful in pretesting programs for adults can certainly be used in pretesting children's programs. It is possible to get an impression of how children will react to a projected program by making a filmstrip with appropriate narration and trying it out on a representative sample of young people of the same age as those for whom the program is intended. The comments made by such previewers are likely to be similar to the comments they would make if they were watching the actual program on a screen.

The filmstrip method of pretesting, although simple, is less valid than a brief segment of the program on film, tape, or kinescope recording. A four-minute segment of a half-hour program would be enough to get reactions to the movement, set, performers, and format from a sample of young viewers. Such a sequence is best projected on a screen size comparable to that of a television screen. By the use of these and similar procedures, a good deal of the guesswork involved in anticipating these reactions to children's programs may be eliminated.

*   *   *

As with any other art form, it is never possible to be completely confident about how the audience will respond to a finished product. There is no doubt, however, that the keener the programmer's awareness of the aspects of the child's world that have been discussed here, the greater will be the response of the young viewer. These aspects represent an irreducible minimum of the kinds of considerations that represent both a challenge and an opportunity for television.

The programmer has access to a huge body of knowledge about the child audience, and he has an obligation to tap this knowledge. Children were the first devoted viewers. They were at least partly responsible for so many parents buying television receivers. Television is reaching young people during the "prime time" of their development, and the attitudes they form toward the medium will condition their subsequent viewing. In the last analysis, programs for the child will be worthy of the interest that the child invests in television only to the extent that creativity and talent as well as knowledge are applied to the "something very different" that is the world of the young viewer.

References

Part I of this section consists of a selected bibliography of books and catalogs in which those interested in programming for children may find sources of film and, in some cases, video tape material that can be used in children's programs.

Part II contains a partial listing of recent books and articles on subjects related to child development and television.

I. Sources of Film Material

Broadcast Information Bureau: *TV Film Source Book,* The Bureau, New York, Fall–Winter, 1961, and Spring Supplement, 1962. A detailed catalog, published annually, of program material cleared for television which is available on film or video tape. Entries are categorized by subject matter and by running time. Names and addresses of producers and distributors are included.

————: *TV "Free" Film Source Book,* The Bureau, New York, Spring–Summer, 1962. A descriptive directory, published annually, of free film available for showing on television from business, governmental, tourist, educational, foundation, and other such sources.

Cross, A. J. Foy, and Irene F. Cypher: *Audio-Visual Education,* Thomas Y. Crowell Company, New York, 1961. A directory of sources of films, filmstrips, flannel-board and other appropriate supplies and materials is contained in an appendix.

Educational Film Library Association: *Films for Children,* The Association, New York, 1961. An annotated list of 205 films selected for entertainment and "literary" values. Criteria for selection are similar to those for choosing good children's books.

National Association of Broadcasters: *Program Material Available from Government and Civic Agencies for Use by Television Stations,* The Association, Washington, 1962. A booklet listing sources of film program and "spot" material. Copies may be ordered by television members of NAB.

Rufsvold, Margaret I., and Carolyn Guss: *Guides to Newer Educational Media,* American Library Association, Chicago, 1961. This publication contains an annotated directory of media catalogs and lists, generally available, with information about their contents, sources, and costs.

United Nations Educational, Scientific and Cultural Organization: *World Film Directory,* UNESCO, Paris, 1962 (UNESCO Publications Center, New York). A directory describing the activities of agencies concerned with educational, scientific, and cultural films throughout the world.

U. S. Department of Health, Education, and Welfare, Office of Education: *A Directory of 3660 16mm Film Libraries,* 1958. A state-by-state and city-by-city list of sources from which films can be borrowed or rented.

————: *U. S. Government Films for Public Educational Use,* 1960. Directory of titles, descriptions, and sources of films produced by agencies of the Federal government or for which the government has major distribution rights. Films that are cleared for television use are so identified.

Wilson (H. W.) Company: *Educational Film Guide,* 11th rev. ed., New York, 1953. Five-year cumulated supplement, 1954-1958; annual supplements, 1959 to date. The definitive catalog of 16mm educational, documentary, travel, and industrial films. Does not include teaching films intended for professional use in medicine, dentistry, public health, and psychiatry. 1954-1958 and subsequent editions omit fiction and Government films.

Wittich, Walter Arno, and Charles Francis Schuller: *Audiovisual Materials: Their Nature and Use,* Harper & Brothers, New York, 1962. An appendix of source lists includes those for film. Some sources other than those in Cross and Cypher *(above)* are named.

II. Child Development, Children and Television, and Related Subjects

Arbuthnot, May Hill: *Children and Books,* Scott, Foresman and Company, Chicago, 1957.

Bramall, Eric: *Puppet Plays and Playwriting,* G. Bell & Sons, London, 1961.

Buhler, Karl: *The Mental Development of the Child,* Harcourt, Brace & World, New York, 1931.

Collier, Mary J.: "The Psychological Appeal in the Cinderella Theme," *American Imago,* 18:399–410, 1961.

Field, Mary: "Children and Films," *Journal of the Royal Society of Arts,* 105:332–343, 1957.

————: *Good Company: The Story of the Children's Entertainment Film Movement in Great Britain, 1943–50,* Longmans Green & Co., Ltd., London, 1952.

Foundation for Character Education, *Television for Children,* The Foundation, Boston, 1962.

Frank, Josette: *Children and TV,* Public Affairs Committee, New York, 1962.

————: *Television: How to Use it Wisely with Children,* Child Study Association of America, New York, 1959.

Gesell, Arnold, and Frances L. Ilg: *The Child from Five to Ten,* Harper & Brothers, New York, 1946.

Harris, Dale B.: *Children and Television: An Annotated Bibliography,* National Association of Educational Broadcasters, Urbana, 1959.

Hazard, Paul: *Books, Children, and Men,* Horn Books, Inc., Boston, 1944.

Himmelweit, Hilde, A. N. Oppenheim, and P. Vince: *Television and the Child,* Oxford University Press, New York, 1958.

Lindstrom, Miriam: *Children's Art,* University of California Press, Berkeley, 1959.

Opie, Iona, and Peter Opie: *The Lore and Language of Schoolchildren,* Oxford University Press, New York, 1959.

Peller, Lili: "Daydreams and Children's Favorite Books," *Psychoanalytic Study of the Child,* 14:414–433, 1959.

Piaget, Jean: *The Child's Conception of the World,* Littlefield, Adams & Co., Paterson, N. J., 1960.

————: *Judgment and Reasoning in the Child,* Littlefield, Adams & Co., Paterson, N. J., 1960.

Pickard, P. M.: *I Could a Tale Unfold,* Humanities Press, New York, 1961.

Schramm, Wilbur, J. Lyle, and E. B. Parker: *Television in the Lives of Our Children,* Stanford University Press, Stanford, Calif., 1961.

Sullivan, Harry Stack: *The Interpersonal Theory of Psychiatry,* W. W. Norton & Company, Inc., New York, 1953.

Winick, Charles: "Satire, Teenagers, and *Mad,*" *Merrill Palmer Quarterly,* 8:183–203, 1962.

Witty, Paul: "Televiewing by Children and Youth," *Elementary English,* 38:103–113, 1961.

List of Stations

The programs described in this survey were reported by the stations listed below. This list does not, however, include those stations producing programs for children that were designed primarily for in-school viewing or for use as an integral part of the school curriculum.

A

Albany, Georgia, WALB-TV
Albany, New York, WAST, W-TEN
Albuquerque, New Mexico,
   *KNME-TV, KOB-TV
Altoona, Pennsylvania, WFBG-TV
Atlanta, Georgia, WAGA-TV, WLW-A
Austin, Texas, KTBC-TV

B

Baltimore, Maryland, WJZ-TV,
   WMAR-TV
Bangor, Maine, WABI-TV
Baton Rouge, Louisiana, WAFB-TV,
   WBRZ
Beaumont, Texas, KFDM-TV
Binghamton, New York, WNBF-TV
Birmingham, Alabama, WBRC-TV
Bloomington, Indiana, WTTV
Boise, Idaho, KTVB
Boston, Massachusetts, WBZ-TV,
   WHDH-TV
Bristol, Virginia, WCYB-TV
Buffalo, New York, WBEN-TV, WGR-TV,
   WKBW-TV
Burlington, Vermont, WCAX-TV

C

Cedar Rapids, Iowa, WMT-TV
Champaign, Illinois, WCIA
Charleston, South Carolina, WCSC-TV
Charlotte, North Carolina, WSOC-TV
Chicago, Illinois, WBBM-TV, WBKB,
   WGN-TV, *WTTW
Chico, California, KHSL-TV
Cincinnati, Ohio, WKRC-TV, WLW-T
Cleveland, Ohio, KYW-TV, WEWS
Colorado Springs, Colorado, KKTV

Columbia, South Carolina, WIS-TV
Columbus, Georgia, WTVM
Columbus, Ohio, WBNS-TV, WLW-C,
   *WOSU-TV, WTVN-TV

D

Dallas, Texas, KRLD-TV, WFAA-TV
Davenport, Iowa, WOC-TV
Dayton, Ohio, WHIO-TV, WLW-D
Denver, Colorado, KLZ-TV, KOA-TV
Des Moines, Iowa, WHO-TV
Detroit, Michigan, WJBK-TV, WWJ-TV,
   WXYZ-TV
Durham, North Carolina, WTVD

E

Eugene, Oregon, KEZI-TV
Evansville, Indiana, WFIE-TV

F

Fairbanks, Alaska, KTVF
Fargo, North Dakota, KXGO-TV
Flint, Michigan, WJRT
Florence, Alabama, WOWL-TV
Fort Dodge, Iowa, KQTV
Fort Wayne, Indiana, WKJG-TV, WPTA
Fort Worth, Texas, WBAP-TV
Fresno, California, KFRE-TV, KJEO

G

Grand Junction, Colorado, KREX-TV
Grand Rapids, Michigan, WOOD-TV
Great Falls, Montana, KRTV
Green Bay, Wisconsin, WFRV, WLUK-TV
Greensboro, North Carolina, WFMY-TV
Greenville, North Carolina, WNCT
Greenville, South Carolina, WFBC-TV

ETV station

H

Harrisonburg, Virginia, WSVA-TV
Hartford, Connecticut, WTIC-TV
Helena, Montana, KBLL-TV
Honolulu, Hawaii, KHVH-TV
Houston, Texas, KHOU-TV, KPRC-TV,
  KTRK-TV
Huntington, West Virginia, WHTN-TV,
  WSAZ-TV

I

Idaho Falls, Idaho, KID-TV
Indianapolis, Indiana, WFBM-TV,
  WISH-TV, WLW-I

J

Jackson, Mississippi, WJTV, WLBT
Jacksonville, Florida, WJXT
Johnstown, Pennsylvania, WJAC-TV

K

Kalamazoo, Michigan, WKZO-TV
Kansas City, Missouri, KCMO-TV,
  WDAF-TV
Knoxville, Tennessee, WBIR-TV

L

La Crosse, Wisconsin, WKBT
Lansing, Michigan, WJIM-TV
Laurel, Mississippi, WDAM-TV
Lexington, Kentucky, WKYT
Lincoln, Nebraska, KOLN-TV
Little Rock, Arkansas, KATV
Los Angeles, California, KABC-TV
  KNXT, KRCA, KTLA
Louisville, Kentucky, WHAS-TV

M

Madison, Wisconsin, WKOW-TV
Marquette, Michigan, WLUC-TV
Mason City, Iowa, KGLO-TV
Memphis, Tennessee, WMCT
Miami, Florida, WCKT, WLBW-TV
Milwaukee, Wisconsin, WITI-TV,
  *WMVS-TV, WTMJ-TV
Minneapolis, Minnesota, WCCO-TV,
  WTCN-TV, KSTP-TV

Mobile, Alabama, WALA-TV, WKRG-TV
Monroe, Louisiana, KNOE-TV
Montgomery, Alabama, WSFA-TV

N

Nashville, Tennessee, WSM-TV
New Britain, Connecticut, WHNB-TV
New Haven, Connecticut, WNHC-TV
New Orleans, Louisiana, WDSU-TV,
  WWL-TV
New York City, New York, WNBC-TV,
  WNEW-TV
Norfolk, Virginia, WAVY-TV, WVEC-TV

O

Oklahoma City, Oklahoma, KWTV,
  WKY-TV
Omaha, Nebraska, KETV, KMTV,
  WOW-TV
Onondaga, Michigan, WILX-TV
Orlando, Florida, WDBO-TV, WLOF-TV

P

Parkersburg, West Virginia, WTAP-TV
Peoria, Illinois, WMBD-TV
Philadelphia, Pennsylvania, WCAU-TV,
  WFIL-TV, WRCV-TV
Phoenix, Arizona, KOOL-TV, KPHO-TV,
  KTAR-TV
Pittsburgh, Pennsylvania, KDKA-TV,
  WIIC, *WQED, WTAE
Poland Spring, Maine, WMTW-TV
Portland, Maine, WCSH-TV, WGAN-TV
Portland, Oregon, KGW-TV, KOIN-TV
Providence, Rhode Island, WJAR-TV,
  WPRO-TV

R

Raleigh, North Carolina, WRAL-TV
Richmond, Virginia, WRVA-TV
Roanoke, Virginia, WDBJ-TV
Rochester, Minnesota, KROC-TV
Rochester, New York, WHEC-TV,
  WROC-TV

S

Sacramento, California, KCRA-TV, KXTV
St. Joseph, Missouri, KFEQ-TV
St. Louis, Missouri, KMOX-TV, KSD-TV, KTVI
St. Paul, Minnesota, *KTCA-TV
Salt Lake City, Utah, KSL-TV, KUTV
San Angelo, Texas, KCTV
San Diego, California, KFMB-TV, KOGO-TV
San Francisco, California, KPIX, *KQED, KRON-TV
Schenectady, New York, WRGB
Scranton, Pennsylvania, WDAU-TV, WNEP-TV
Seattle, Washington, *KCTS-TV, KING-TV, KIRO-TV, KOMO-TV
Shreveport, Louisiana, KSLA-TV, KTBS-TV
Sioux City, Iowa, KVTV
Sioux Falls, South Dakota, KELO-TV
South Bend, Indiana, WNDU-TV, WSBT-TV, WSJV-TV
Spokane, Washington, KHQ-TV, KXLY-TV
Springfield, Illinois, WICS-TV
Springfield, Massachusetts, WHYN-TV
Syracuse, New York, WHEN-TV, WSYR-TV

T

Tacoma, Washington, KTVW
Tallahassee, Florida, WCTV
Tampa, Florida, WFLA-TV, WTVT
Terre Haute, Indiana, WTHI-TV
Toledo, Ohio, WSPD-TV, WTOL-TV
Topeka, Kansas, WIBW-TV
Tucson, Arizona, KOLD-TV
Tulsa, Oklahoma, KOTV, KVOO-TV

U

Utica, New York, WKTV

V

Valley City, North Dakota, KXJB-TV

W

Washington, D.C., WTOP-TV
West Palm Beach, Florida, WEAT-TV
Wheeling, West Virginia, WTRF-TV
Wichita, Kansas, KTVH
Winston-Salem, North Carolina, WSJS-TV

Y

York, Pennsylvania, WSBA-TV
Youngstown, Ohio, WKBN-TV

The Television Information Office was activated in March, 1959, by resolution of the Television Board of Directors of the National Association of Broadcasters. In October, 1959, the Office was opened to form a two-way bridge between the industry and its many publics. It receives financial support from individual television stations, the three nationwide television networks, and the National Association of Broadcasters.